TEACHING
AMOS

Unlocking the Prophecy of Amos
for the Bible Teacher

BOB FYALL

SERIES EDITORS: DAVID JACKMAN & ROBIN SYDSERFF

D1637574

CHRISTIAN FOCUS

Rev. Dr. Bob Fyall is the Director of Rutherford House, Edinburgh, a centre for theological study and research. Prior to that he taught Old Testament in Cranmer Hall, St John's College, Durham while pastoring a church where a large student ministry developed. His previous writings include a Focus on the Bible Commentary on *Daniel* (ISBN 1-84550-194-5).

Copyright © Proclamation Trust Media 2006

ISBN 1-84550-142-X
ISBN 978-1-84550-142-6

10 9 8 7 6 5 4 3 2 1

Published in 2006
by
Christian Focus Publications,
Geanies House, Fearn,
Ross-shire, IV20 1TW, Scotland, Great Britain
with
Proclamation Trust Media,
Willcox House, 140-148 Borough High Street,
London, SE1 1LB, England, Great Britain.
www.proctrust.org.uk

www.christianfocus.com

Cover design by Moose77.com
Printed and bound by Nørhaven Paperback A/S, Denmark

Contents

Other Books in the *Teach the Bible* Series include:

Teaching John
by Dick Lucas and William Philip
(ISBN 1-85792-790-7)

Teaching Matthew
by David Jackman and William Philip
(ISBN 1-85792-877-6)

Teaching the Christian Hope
by David Jackman
(ISBN 1-85792-518-1)

SERIES PREFACE

Whether you are a preacher, a small group Bible study leader or a youth worker, the *Teach the Bible* Series will be an ideal companion in your study. Few commentaries are written specifically with the preacher or the Bible teacher in mind, and with the sermon or Bible talk as the point of reference. The preacher or teacher, the sermon or talk and the listener are the 'key' drivers in this series. The books are purposely practical, seeking to offer real help for those involved in teaching biblical material to others. The aim is to help the Bible teacher get to grips with the text, with its intended purpose clearly in view – its proclamation as the living Word of God. The series is strategically positioned to complement the Bible commentaries. Commentaries are an essential resource for the serious Bible teacher and accordingly, each book will include a synopsis/guide to the best of them.

There are a number of specific features common to the books in this series. The opening chapter offers an overview of the biblical book or doctrinal theme ('Getting Our Bearings in Amos'), identifying key themes, structure, literary style etc.

Issues pertinent to preaching and teaching the material are a key focus of this navigation chapter. For example, *Teaching Amos* includes a section on dealing with repetition in Scripture, a particular feature of the prophetic literature. The opening chapter concludes with a number of suggestions as to how the material might best be divided for a preaching or teaching series. These range from expository series that cover the entire biblical book, to shorter series on sections of the text. Having identified a number of possible approaches, one of the whole book series is selected as the basis for the meat of the *Teaching* book. Individual chapters correspond with individual sermons or talks. The content is neither commentary nor sermon, but rather expositions for expositors or teachers. The material is specifically geared toward working from text to sermon or talk, combining rigorous exposition with relevant application, always with an eye to the main teaching point of the passage. At the end of each chapter, a short section, entitled 'Preaching and Teaching Notes', suggests one or more outline structures for a sermon or talk. These sections also contain discussions of pertinent issues for the preacher or Bible teacher. For example, *Teaching Amos* includes a helpful excursus on 'Preaching on Judgement'. Indeed we trust that under God, one of the major contributions of this book will be a recovery of nerve amongst preachers to preach judgement fairly and squarely.

Teaching Amos is written by Dr Bob Fyall, who has a wealth of experience in preaching and teaching the Old Testament. Bob is a scholar and writer but, above all, he is a passionate preacher of this material. It is our prayer that this volume will encourage better preaching on Amos in particular, and the prophetic literature in general, confident in the striking relevance of the prophet's message for today.

David Jackman and Robin Sydserff, Series Editors
London, March 2006

AUTHOR'S PREFACE

In whatever context you are preaching or teaching the Bible, this book is written with your needs in view. Its primary focus is to facilitate preaching and teaching on Amos in particular, and on the Old Testament prophetic literature in general. Unlocking this material yields a wealth of rich and relevant resources.

The book of Amos is a good way to get into systematic exposition of the Old Testament prophets. It is short enough to tackle in a relatively brief space of time yet it grapples with major issues and anticipates in smaller compass the great prophets, such as Isaiah and Jeremiah. Above all, it is a book that brings us face to face with God in a life-changing encounter. Our authority and example for preaching the Old Testament comes from the Lord Jesus Christ himself. Jesus' words on the road to Emmaus are striking: 'And beginning with Moses and all the Prophets, he interpreted to them in all the Scriptures the things concerning himself' (Luke 24:27). We cannot understand Christ unless we engage with the Old Testament. As preachers and Bible teachers we have a responsibility to facilitate people's engagement with the whole Bible.

While this is not an exhaustive exposition of Amos, all sections of the book are covered in some detail. Amos' book has a marked simplicity in its focus on three great themes: the God who Speaks, the God of Creation and the God of History. At the same time it embodies rich variety, exploring these themes from different angles and presenting them in different styles.

This book will be best used after the preacher or Bible teacher has done some hard work on the text using the kind of commentaries mentioned in the Appendix. Commentaries are seldom geared specifically to the preacher or teacher and *Teaching Amos*, like others in the series, is designed to help those who need guidance on how to organise the material for effective preaching. The concern is always to listen to the voice of God through the words of Amos and proclaim it as the living Word of God.

The conviction of this series is that the whole Bible is the Word of God and that through the written Word we meet the living Word, Christ Jesus. Thus, the aim is to help preachers not simply to understand the text in an academic sense, but to so allow that Word to become part of themselves so that they will be better able to feed those to whom they preach, whether in sermons or in individual conversations. My hope and prayer is that many will be inspired to preach and teach Amos, appreciating the power and timely relevance of its message.

Bob Fyall
Edinburgh, March 2006

I

GETTING OUR BEARINGS IN AMOS

In this introductory chapter we shall explore six major issues which will provide a foundation for the detailed work on the text of Amos that follows.

(1) Amos and Prophecy

Amos comes from that large section of the Old Testament known as the 'Writing Prophets', often referred to simply as 'the Prophets'. This section begins with Isaiah, Jeremiah and Ezekiel and is followed by the Book of the Twelve (Hosea, Joel, Amos etc. through to Malachi). The term 'Minor Prophets' is often used as an alternative to 'the Book of the Twelve' in order to reflect their relative length compared to Isaiah, Jeremiah and Ezekiel, is unhelpful, as it could imply their relative insignificance. Nothing could be further from the truth! As we read and preach Amos, and the other books from Hosea to Malachi, we shall find that we are grappling with great truths of striking contemporary relevance.

Arguably, the dominant melodic line in the Prophets is the divine view of history and of God's judgements both *in* and *on* history. A key-note is the 'Day of the Lord'. As we interpret the Prophets, we must understand that they present God as the Lord of Creation and the Lord of History, who will one day bring in a new heaven and a new earth.[1]

Three markers will help us to place the Prophets in general and Amos in particular into sharper focus.

(i)   *The significance of Moses*

The first is the significance of Moses in the prophetic literature. Moses is the fountainhead of Old Testament revelation. He is the unique prophet whom God knew face to face (Deut. 34:10). Through him was given the Torah (Pentateuch), the most basic and fundamental part of the Old Testament. The words of Moses are the words of God; there is no revelation in Old Testament times which is superior to and independent of that given to Moses. The fact that his name is not mentioned by the prophets all that often is not particularly significant; their words presuppose the Sinai Covenant and often they quote or allude to the Pentateuch (e.g. Amos 2:4). Thus the prophets are raised up to call people back to the message given to Moses as the way to build godly lives and flourishing communities. That is why the term 'man of God' is frequently used of such people. Moses is the man of God *par excellence* and those who speak for God draw their inspiration from him. When they speak, their words are consistent with the earlier revelation.

This revelation to Moses was faithfully followed by Joshua and the elders who outlived him (Joshua 24:31), but thereafter continual apostasy is chronicled in the book of Judges. God raised up Samuel (1 Sam. 3), an enormously significant figure who called the nation back to God. Then in the ninth century BC Elijah bursts onto the scene (1 Kings 17), and from then until 2 Kings 13, the text is dominated by Elijah and his disciple Elisha. They speak the true message of God and attack Baalism and syncretism. Along with these 'big' figures there are a number of 'individual appearances' of both anonymous and named prophets (such as Micaiah in 1 Kings 22). They keep the Word of God before the people until the appearance of the first of the prophets, Amos and Hosea, who warn of the coming judgement. The message of Amos is, therefore, central to the ongoing revelation in Scripture.

(ii)   *The authentic voice of the prophet*

Secondly, it is important that we are clear on how we recognise the true prophet and the authentic prophetic voice. False prophets misled people (Deut. 13:2, 3; 18:20; Jer. 2:8; 23:26, 27), lived ungodly lives (Jer. 23:14) and often practised magic (Isa. 8:19; Jer. 14:14). Frequently the term 'prophet' was a derogatory one (Jer. 2:8; 5:13, 31; 23:30-31; Amos 7:14). The words of the genuine prophet are not only his own words (Amos 1:1) but also the Word of the Lord (Amos 1:2). This Word is received by them; it did not originate in themselves. Moreover, the true prophet is one who is called. Many of these calls are described (e.g. Exod. 1; 1 Sam. 3; Isa. 6; Jer. 1; Ezek. 1; and Amos 7:14). Even where such a call is not specifically mentioned, authenticity is clearly established by the fact that the prophet brings the Word of Yahweh to the people. And yet, there is need for discernment. For example, in 1 Kings 22:11, Zedekiah, the false prophet, claims to have heard the voice of the Lord as often as the true prophet Micaiah (1 Kings 22: 19-20).

(iii)   *Apostolic understanding of the prophetic message*

Thirdly, it is helpful to have in mind the significance of 2 Peter 1:19-21 in understanding the prophetic message. Peter's teaching not only reminds us of the divine nature of the prophetic voice when they spoke of Christ's coming (ratified in the transfiguration which he recalls in vv. 16-18), but also of their continued relevance alongside the apostolic testimony. The Old and New Testament revelations are two stages in God's *ongoing* revelation of his purposes. We still need the words of the prophets, and must continue to read and preach them, because they are our light in the darkness of the world 'until the day dawns and the morning star arises in your hearts' (2 Peter 1:19b). The Old Testament remains the living Word of God until Christ returns, when all that the prophets said will be proved to be authentic. Therefore, we preach Amos in the confidence that as we do so, we are shining the light of God into the surrounding darkness.

(2) Who was Amos?

Amos is described as one 'who was among the shepherds of Tekoa' (Amos 1:1). This has led some commentators to a rather sentimentalised view of Amos as a simple, rustic figure declaiming against the evils of the 'big city'. Such a view undermines the impact of his words, reducing them to trite moralizing. The description used of Amos would more probably suggest an owner of flocks. Moreover, his message was nothing to do with town versus country and everything to do with hearing God's voice across the entire socio-geographical spectrum. It is clear that Amos had a wide knowledge of the social and political issues of his time and a grasp of the international situation (e.g. Amos 1:3–2:3 and chs 3–6). But above all, he had a powerful sensitivity concerning the unacceptability of Israel's religious life. Some of the most eloquent passages in the book attack insincerity, hypocrisy and a failure to meet with and listen to God (e.g. Amos 4:4-5; 5:21-26).

(3) When did Amos Minister?

Amos states clearly when he spoke his message – sometime in the reigns of Uzziah of Judah (791-740 BC) and Jeroboam II of Israel (793-753 BC)[2]. The exile of Israel at the hands of Assyria took place c. 722 BC. The time of Amos' ministry is more precisely defined as 'two years before the earthquake' (Amos 1:1b), which suggests that he prophesied during a relatively brief period (the earthquake is remembered in Zechariah 14:5 some centuries later which shows how significant an event it was).

Both Uzziah and Jeroboam II were able kings (see 2 Chronicles 26 for Uzziah and 2 Kings 14:23-29 for Jeroboam II). However, in their reigns two big problems begin to emerge: the rise of Assyria as a super-power, coupled with internal socio-economic problems. We shall see evidence of both of those problems in Amos.

(4) Amos' Message

Just as the Gentile nations would be judged for their wickedness, so also Israel and Judah will be judged. Although in Amos chapter 2 (vv. 4-16), 'Judah' and 'Israel' are used in a geographical sense (where oracles are addressed to the Southern and Northern Kingdoms), in the rest of the book (from 3:1 onwards), Israel is used to refer to the whole people of God. Amos' ministry reveals the severity of God's judgement against his chosen people and yet declares the hope of restoration after the coming destruction and exile. The exile/exodus motif is a strong theme in Amos.

It is helpful at this point to see the book in its outline structure. It comprises a number of oracles and visions.[3] The oracles, which Amos probably delivered at different times during the brief period of his public ministry, constitute the bulk of the book (1:3–6:14; 9:11-15). Between the concentrated block of oracles and the concluding oracle, Amos reports five visions of judgement on Israel (7:1– 9:10).

(i)   *The oracles*

The first series of oracles (1:3-2:16) opens with judgement on the surrounding nations (1:3-2:3), before focusing on God's chosen people, first Judah (2:4-5) and then an opening summary indictment against Israel (2:6-16). The section from 3:1-5:14 comprises five separate oracles. The first three oracles are announcement oracles ('Hear this word...' (3:1; 4:1; 5:1)), which pronounce, with justification and illustration, the coming judgement on Israel. The third of these takes the form of a lament and call to repentance (5:1-17). The announcement oracles are followed by two woe oracles ('Woe to you...' (5:18; 6:1)) which reflect on how Israel has lapsed into a complacency that is rooted in the false security of religious practice (5:18-27), military success and material possessions (6:1-14). The book closes with an oracle of salvation pronouncing Israel's restoration (9:11-15). Chapter 5 is not only the literary centre of the book, but also the thematic centre. The chiastic structure

(5:1-17), beginning and ending with a lament over Israel's fall, is particularly striking.

(ii) *The visions*

The section from 7:1-9:10 comprises five visions of judgement. In 7:1-9 Amos reports three visions: the locusts (vv. 1-3), the fire (vv. 4-6) and the plumb line (vv. 7-9). This is followed by the insertion into the book of a narrative account of Amos' encounter with Amaziah, the priest of Bethel (i.e. the king's priest) (vv. 10-17). This narrative insertion illustrates both opposition to the content of Amos' message and Amos' faithfulness in conveying his God-given message, in spite of the opposition. In chapter eight, Amos reports the vision of the basket of ripe fruit (8:1-3), which he then elaborates on through a series of judgement oracles (8:4-14). The final vision (9:1-10) is of Yahweh standing by the altar at Bethel; a vision of utter destruction.

Included within the oracles and visions are three doxologies (4:13; 5:8-9 and 9:5-6). Finally in terms of overall structure, the first two verses of chapter 1 are identifiable as a separate section, giving us the key to understanding the book. The emphases in these verses are developed and amplified in various ways throughout the text. These introductory verses offer an ideal focal point for an opening sermon, and accordingly are the subject of extended treatment in chapter 2.

Notwithstanding the wide and rich variety of literary forms that characterize the text, Amos has a powerful underlying unity in terms of its overall message – the awesomeness and inescapability of the God of the Covenant who governs the nations in righteousness and judgement.

Amos in outline:

(1) Introduction:
God, the Word and its Consequences *(1:1-2)*

(2) Oracles:
Oracles Against the Nations: the surrounding Nations, Judah and Israel *(1:3–2:16)*

- *(i)   The surrounding nations (1:3–2:3)*
- *(ii)   Judah (2:4-5)*
- *(iii) Israel (2:6-16)*

Judgement Oracles on Israel *(3:1–6:14)*

- *(i)   Announcement oracle 1 (3:1-15)*
- *(ii)   Announcement oracle 2 (including doxology 1) (4:1-13)*
- *(iii) Announcement oracle 3 (in the form of a lament (including doxology 2)) (5:1-17)*
- *(iv)   Woe oracle 1 (5:18-27)*
- *(v)   Woe oracle 2 (6:1-14)*

(3) Visions:
Visions of Judgement on Israel *(7:1–9:10)*

- *(i)   Vision of the locusts (7:1-3)*
- *(ii)   Vision of the fire (7:4-6)*
- *(iii) Vision of the plumb line (7:7-9)*
      Narrative insertion – Amos' encounter with Amaziah (7:10-17)
- *(iv)   Vision of the basket of ripe fruit (8:1-3)*
      Elaboration on vision - judgement oracle (8:4-14)
- *(v)   Vision of God standing at the altar (including doxology 3) (9:1-10)*

(4) Final Oracle:
Oracle of Salvation for Israel *(9:11-15)*

(5) Preaching Christ from Amos

One reason why the Old Testament is often neglected in our preaching is that we fear we will not make the gospel clear enough. This evidences a misunderstanding of what the gospel is. The gospel is the whole written Word, which faithfully and fully presents the living Word, Christ Jesus. We must have this clear. As we expound the text (whether from the Old or New Testaments) we are preaching the gospel. Indeed, our gospel preaching is *most articulate* when we expound the text.

We must not preach the Old Testament ignoring the genuine historical setting and the actual personal experiences of both the author and the first listeners and readers; yet we need to take account of the New Testament witness to Christ and relate that to the earlier stage of revelation in the Old Testament. Christ is *the* revelation of the God whom Amos preaches; his coming will usher in the Day of the Lord and his kingdom will be what Israel failed to be. More particularly, the Lord who roars from Zion is the one who, as the Lion of Judah, will pronounce judgement on history. He is also the one whose kingdom will abolish social injustice and the oppression of the poor. He will rebuild 'David's fallen tent' (Amos 9:11), and as his Greater Son, will rule in Zion. As we grasp these realities we can begin to do justice both to Amos in his own time and see him as part of the prophetic Scriptures which were used by Christ himself to expound the significance of his death and resurrection (Luke 24:25-27).

(6) Planning a Preaching Series on Amos

In this final introductory section let me say something first about Amos the preacher, second, about how we should deal in our preaching with prophetic repetition, and third, suggest how we might go about planning a preaching series or teaching outline for this book.

(i)   *Amos the preacher*

Amos is giving us words which embody a vision received from God. This is an indication of the importance of the preached Word; this message received in picture must be interpreted and applied. The whole book is shot through with vivid imagery and the appeal is to the heart as well as the mind. This is true in the more straightforward oracles as well as in the visions of chapters 7–9.

Amos is a poet and an artist who uses all the resources of language to make his message as clear as possible. And since he is, above all else, a preacher, he has much to say about the power of the divine Word. He intends his hearers and readers to face the implications of their faith in a way that will leave no part of their hearts and minds unaffected. As preachers we need to realize that our expositions of the Word must be similarly concerned with mind and heart. Preaching is never simply a cerebral exercise. We must avoid collapsing exposition into 'explaining the passage'. Of course the passage must be explained as simply and effectively as possible, and while there must be a clear structure to what we are saying, that is only the beginning. Both heart and soul must be engaged, for preaching is to the whole person. Amos is passionate about his message and uses many different styles and techniques to bring it home to his hearers. A preacher like Amos, whose ministry marries clarity with passion, is an excellent model!

A question which arises here is how Amos organized his material. Some have pointed out that his message is akin to collage, which, both electronically and in print, is a common way of trying to express the essence of an institution or a body by pictures, some text, clips of various kinds and music. The aim is to create a mood and an impression for the would-be audience. There is some truth in this, but we must remember that Amos controls his material and shapes it all to underline his fundamental message of the God who is Lord of Creation, Lord of History and the one who speaks, acts and whose holiness is to be feared. Our confidence then is to preach and teach Amos' material systematically, unlocking the rhythm of Amos' preaching as we do so, reflecting its dynamic shifts in content and tone.

(ii) Dealing with prophetic repetition in applying Amos' message today

An important consideration is how we deal with repetition when preaching on a book like Amos. Repetition is a particular feature of the prophetic literature. The prophet must repeat and reiterate his message in order to penetrate hard and stubborn hearts. It is important in our preaching of this material that we hold firmly to the principle of divine inspiration, not just in terms of content, but also in relation to tone, emphasis and repetition. A close study of the text often reveals that what appears to be simple repetition is, in fact, reiteration and re-emphasis, employing subtle shifts in content and tone. Moreover, the use of different literary forms throughout the text (announcement oracles (including laments), woe oracles, visions and doxologies) creates a rich overall tapestry. Our preaching will be all the more dynamic if it reflects that subtlety and richness.

Equally, however, it is important not to get 'bogged down' in preaching this material, but to work through it at a pace implied by the text. Amos is a perfect illustration of what I mean, where much of the book is a collection of what would originally have been preached material. It is a helpful guiding principle that as we preach it, we should be mindful of how Amos preached it. Take for example the first announcement oracle (3:1-15). One sermon on this section, dealing with the judgement of God, seems more appropriate than three on the fairness (3:1-2), the inevitability (3:3-8) and the comprehensiveness (3:9-15) of God's judgement. A constant challenge for the expository preacher is to bring the weight of repeated prophetic censure to bear on a congregation's life in a way that reflects the repeated content in the text and yet effectively engages the hearer week after week. Preparation involving an initial run through the whole preaching series is essential if the expositor is to reflect the overall balance of repeated teaching in the book, rather than just arbitrarily selecting from the repeated themes that resonate with the expositor. Preparing the whole preaching series (at least in outline) allows the areas of life repeatedly addressed to be identified, and a plan made to major on one or two of the recurring themes as the passages come up in the preaching series. Over the course of the series all the repeated themes can be covered without compromising our commitment to systematic exposition.

For example, in Amos the theme of inappropriate attitude to wealth and poverty occurs in 2:6-8; 3:12,15; 4:1; 5:11; 6:1-7; 8:4-6. It is impossible to deal in depth (in a normal length sermon, at least) with this theme each time it occurs in the passage being expounded, along with the other recurrent themes in the same passage. But rather than touch upon each recurrent theme in each sermon on every text where the themes are mentioned, the preacher can highlight in introducing the series, that the theme of wealth will be addressed at length, for example, in the fifth sermon, and make just a few summary comments in other sermons when the text refers to it. This way the preacher will still reflect something of Amos' prophetic repetition, but also create the context within which each recurrent theme can be applied to the congregation at length. Careful planning of the overall series will allow several recurrent themes to be addressed fully, and their application examined in the light of contemporary issues and concerns. For example: wrong attitudes to wealth and poverty; worship that is repugnant to the Lord; Christian complacency; the meaning of seeking the Lord; the consequences of not proclaiming or listening to the Word of the Lord, etc. The suggested structure for preaching through Amos that I outline in the next section seeks to be faithful to the nature of divine inspiration as it is reflected in the systematic development of Amos' repeated teaching in a way that effectively engages the hearer through the series. What I offer, however, is a starting point. It is for you as the preacher or Bible study leader, familiar with your context, to weight the material in the most appropriate way.

(iii) *Planning a preaching series*

Those who have not preached often on the Prophets will find Amos an ideal book to tackle, both for its own sake and as a way into preaching on the longer prophetic books. In this introductory chapter, I have tried to set out some of the background and the major themes dealt with by Amos. Getting our bearings at the outset on matters of authorship, background, dominant themes and genre, is essential preparation for preaching on any biblical book. Acquiring this knowledge is not, of course, so that we can give a dry lecture on background. That would be like inviting people for a meal and showing them the ingredients laid out on the kitchen table! Rather, we must cook a satisfying dinner using and blending these ingredients.

I want to outline three ways in which we might plan a preaching series on Amos. The first of these will form the material for the rest of this book, but the other two may appeal to some who want to preach on Amos but spend fewer sessions on it. On the matter of titles for series and individual sermons, not everyone committed to expository preaching would subscribe to such an approach, particularly if it involves settling on a structure at the start of a planned preaching programme. That is fair enough; there is no one correct method to be used. In my own preaching over the years, however, I have found that to announce beforehand not only the book to be studied but to give some indication of how you intend to 'travel the territory' is helpful. There are two reasons for this: first, it keeps the preacher firmly bound to the task which has enormous benefits in seeing the terrain as a whole, whatever unexpected treasures may turn up *en route*; second, it helps the hearer to have a sense of a shared journey with identifiable landmarks. The Holy Spirit is as surely able to inspire a whole series as a single sermon.

The titles chosen here are guides not straitjackets. We must always be vigilant to the danger of expounding the title rather than the text! That said, titles are helpful if they capture the main teaching point of the relevant section of biblical text. The best titles will be distilled guides as to how you will approach the passage and it is essential that they are analytical rather than descriptive.[4]

It has already been suggested that the main theme of Amos' message is expressed in 1:1-2, especially the majesty and awesomeness of God. This God is the Lion of Judah whose roar echoes through the whole earth; a God big enough to handle the huge problems of our world, to bring history to a conclusion and create a new heaven and a new earth. Aslan is on the move! "'Safe', said Mrs Beaver, "don't you hear what Mr Beaver tells you? Who said anything about safe? Course he isn't safe. But he's good. He's the King, I tell you.'"[5] No doubt, you'll have anticipated where this is going! I would suggest a series title such as 'Not a Tame Lion'. It is striking and consistent with the nature and tone of Amos (and will also ring some topical literary bells!) When Amos says in 4:12: '...prepare to meet your God', we know that this meeting is going to be an awesome experience, and one which will be life-changing. The book ends with the words '...says the Lord your God' (Amos 9:15b), leaving the reader in no doubt that its promises of judgement and restoration *will be fulfilled*.

Series 1

With this as the overriding thrust of the book we might preach a series of nine sermons. It is helpful to structure this series of nine in three parts, reflecting the melodic line of the text. While these divisions broadly reflect the literary structure of the book, for example, the movement from oracles to visions, the literary forms employed by Amos must not be our primary consideration in dividing up the text. Our concern is always with the melodic line, and on occasions our individual sermons will embrace different literary forms. For example, the final sermon suggested takes the whole of chapter 9, embracing the final vision of judgement and the concluding salvation oracle. *This outline will form the basis for the main section of the book.*

Series title: **'Not a Tame Lion'**
Individual sermons:

Part One: God and the Nations
1. **'The Awesome God'** *(1:1-2)*
    The Lord God of History and Creation speaks

2. **'Calling the Nations to Account'** *(1:3–2:16)*
    The sweep of God's judgement

Part Two: Indictment and Judgement on Israel
3. **'If God is Against Us'** *(3:1-15)*
    The justness of God's judgement

4. **'Prepare to Meet Your God'** *(4:1-13)*
    A catalogue of failures

5. **'Stop Playing at Meetings'** *(5:1-27)*
    False security in religious practices

6. **'Stop Being Complacent'** *(6:1-14)*
    False security in military success and material possessions

Part Three: Visions of Judgement and Hope for Israel
7. **'Seeing It As It Is'** *(7:1-17)*
    Who pulls the strings and who speaks the truth?

8. **'A Famine of the Word of God'** *(8:1-14)*
    The inevitable consequence of judgement

9. **'In Anger Remembering Mercy'** *(9:1-15)*
    Annihilation and restoration

Series 2
If time is more limited, here are two further suggestions; one for six and one for five sermons. The overall title of the series would remain the same.

Series title: 'Not a Tame Lion'
Individual sermons:

1.   **'The Awesome God'** *(1:1-2:16)*
     This would combine the material of sermons 1 and 2 above.

2.   **'If God is Against Us'** *(3:1-15)* (as above)

3.   **'Prepare to Meet Your God'** *(4:1-13)* (as above)

4.   **'Playing With Fire'** *(5:1-6:14)*
     This would combine the material of sermons 5 and 6 above.

5.   **'Seeing It As It Is'** *(7:1-8:14)*
     This would combine the material of sermons 7 and 8 above.

6.   **'In Anger Remembering Mercy'** *(9:1-15)* (as above)

I shall suggest other variations as we go through the book. Both those sermon series cover the entire book and are faithful to the structure and flow of the prophecy.

Series 3
A third way of looking at much of the material in Amos would be a thematic study. Five sermons could be preached:

Series title: 'Not a Tame Lion'
Individual sermons:

1.   **'Amos' God'**

2.   **'Amos' Worship'**

3.   **'Amos and the Word of God'**

4.   **'Amos' Social Concern'**

5.   **'Amos' Visions'**

While thematic studies can be helpful in grasping the overall thrust of a book, it would be unwise for preachers to employ this as a first engagement with Amos or, indeed, any other book. The danger of a thematic study is that a lot of good biblical material can be presented which is not specifically related to the canonical shape of the book. The God of Amos and of Daniel, of Romans and Revelation is the same God, but each author presents God in his unique way. Biblical authors each have their agenda and particular audience in view which, under the Holy Spirit, shape the presentation of their message. Thematic treatment often ignores genre and setting. That said, if you have already preached on Amos and want to try a different approach, then a short thematic series might be appropriate.

But now the ground has been cleared and we are ready to get into the text of Amos.

Endnotes

1. Indeed, this theme is dominant in the books of the Former Prophets (Joshua through Kings (with the exception of Ruth)).

2. Jeroboam II is referred to in this way to distinguish him from Jeroboam I, often called 'Jeroboam, son of Nebat', the first king of Israel who reigned from 930-909 BC (see 1 Kings 12:25–14:20).

3. I include some further notes on the literary and theological features of oracles and visions in chapters 3 and 8, respectively.

4. I owe this point to Alec Motyer.

5. C. S. Lewis, The Lion, the Witch and the Wardrobe (Harper Collins, 3rd Impression, 1992), p.75.

PART ONE:

God and the Nations

Amos 1:1–2:16

2

'The Awesome God'

The Lord God of History and Creation speaks

(Amos 1:1-2)

Introduction

If you ask people today what their view of God is, or more specifically, what we most need to hear about God, the answer would probably be that he is love. That is, of course, fundamental, because if God is not love, then we have no assurance that he will bring about a future that is good and gracious. But here arises another problem. If his love is no more than a well-meaning and friendly disposition, how do we know that he can carry out his purposes? We need to know that God is big enough to fulfil his purpose of creating a new heaven and new earth. It is this God, an awesome and powerful God, whom Amos presents at the beginning of his prophecy.

Two verses may seem a very small passage to preach on, but these verses are packed with great truths, establishing the main themes of Amos that are echoed throughout the book. God, and his powerful intervention in the world, with the kind of preaching that results when such a God is taken seriously, is the great concern of the book. In our preaching on those verses, as suggested in chapter 1, we shall also be able to introduce a number of background points concerning Amos, his time and situation, etc., showing the relevance of these to his message. Very simply, verses 1-2 establish who, when and what, and open the door into this fascinating and disturbing book. In particular, three great truths about God are presented: he is a God who speaks, he is the Lord of History and he is the Lord of Creation. We shall consider each in turn.

(1) God Speaks

There is no more basic truth about the God of the Bible than this; that he speaks. He is a God who acts, but the revelation comes when he unfolds the meaning of events. By contrast, the gods of the nations do not speak; they remain silent and indifferent (see e.g. 1 Kings 18 when the prophets of Baal fail to elicit a response from him, and in Daniel when the representatives of the pagan gods are unable to interpret, let alone recount, dreams). In Amos, there are three ways in which God speaks.

(i)   *God speaks through his messengers*

He speaks first through his messengers: 'The words of Amos, who was among the shepherds of Tekoa...' (v. 1a). The Word which uniquely and fully becomes flesh in Jesus, becomes flesh also, in a secondary sense, in his messengers. 'The words of Amos' show that this is no disembodied communication; these are the words of a real man who speaks the same basic message as his contemporary, Hosea, yet has his own distinctive style. As already noted, Amos is in all probability an owner of flocks rather than a simple shepherd. Moreover, the message he brings has nothing to do with country versus town, but everything to do with God. He is an orator of great power, a poet and a penetrating critic of all sham and unreality. His public ministry, or at least that recorded in the Bible, must have been brief. The phrase 'two years before the earthquake' (v. 1b) suggests a period of under a year. This is a useful reminder that a ministry's value does not depend on its length. It has all to do with God's purposes and timing.

(ii)   God speaks in visions and words

God speaks, secondly, in a vision which is also a word. Notice the parallelism: 'The words of Amos... which he saw' (v. 1a). Amos was given a true vision of reality by the Lord and his book is a distillation of that vision, including some accounts of visions in chapters 7-9. This gives us an insight into the nature of revelation. The prophet is one who stands in the divine counsel and sees a vision of God and the world (e.g. Isa. 6). He then translates that vision into words, words which have living and transforming power. Both elements are essential. The prophet needs to see not only the outward circumstances but the reality of the unseen Lord and the invisible world. He then conveys that reality, not by drawing pictures, but by speaking. We shall examine further the relationship of vision and word in our discussion of Amos chapters 7-9.

(iii)   God speaks directly into the world

Thirdly, God speaks directly into the world he has created. Two significant verbs are used in verse 2. First, he 'roars' from Zion. The verb used there is not the contented purr of the lion at the end of a good meal. This is the pouncing roar of the lion as it launches itself on its prey.[1] This God is terrifying and likely to cause total upheaval in any situation in which he intervenes. His voice cannot be ignored. He is not a tame lion! The other verb, translated 'thunders' in the NIV, is literally 'gives his voice' (the ESV has 'utters his voice'). In chapter 3:7 we are to hear further of God's secret voice to 'his servants the prophets', but this is a public and spectacular utterance. The thunder of God's voice is heard elsewhere in Scripture in passages such as Job 37:2 and Psalm 29:3-5, 7-9. It is also characteristic of theophany passages such as Psalm 18 and Habakkuk 3. Taken together, these words reinforce the awesome and challenging nature of the God of Amos. It is this awesome power of God that lies behind Amos' concern throughout the book to cause his hearers to comprehend the nature of the Lord whom they despise and whose laws they break.

There is much that is instructive for us here as we preach on the importance of hearing the voice of God. The contemporary preacher listens to the words of Amos which are the Word of God and preaches these words believing that the same power is present. This is not to say that the preacher is inspired in the same direct way as the prophet, but that he becomes a channel of that same living Word which speaks not only into Amos' time but into every other age.

Having established first that God is a God who speaks, and the urgent necessity is to heed that voice, these introductory verses also reveal in summary form the content of Amos' message. That content is centred on two fundamental Old Testament themes: God is the Lord of History and God is the Lord of Creation.

(2) God is Lord of History

One of the great historians of the early twentieth century, H. A. L. Fisher, wrote: 'Men wiser and more learned than I have discerned in history a plot, a rhythm, a predetermined pattern. These harmonies are concealed from me. I can see only one emergency following upon another, as wave follows upon wave.'[2] Amos' conviction, however, is that history has a clear purpose because Yahweh is Lord of History. It is helpful to see Yahweh's intervention in history both particularly and generally. By particular, we mean his particular intervention at particular times, because of particular circumstances. By general, we understand that God's particular intervention in history is caught up in his grand plan of salvation history. Failure to embrace these perspectives will result in our failure to grasp that the specific circumstances in which Amos, (or any other biblical writer) speaks, have meaning and significance beyond their time.

(i)   God's particular intervention in salvation history

Amos fixes the time of his message as 'two years before the earthquake' (v. 1b), and the severe earthquake which struck the town of Hazor between 765 and 760 BC is a possible context. The severity and significance of this earthquake is witnessed to in Zechariah 14:5 where it is seen as a harbinger of the Last Day. Plainly the earthquake was part of the judgement Amos announces. He further dates his message in the reigns of two kings: Uzziah of Judah (791-740 BC) of whom a fuller picture is given in 2 Chronicles 26; and Jeroboam II of Israel (793-753 BC), (see 2 Kings 14:23-29). Both were able kings, during whose reigns their countries enjoyed a kind of Indian summer of peace and prosperity. They may not be household names to us, but the prophet deliberately draws attention to them, and by so doing he hints at what are to be his main concerns as he speaks God's Word to his contemporaries.

Two issues were emerging as Hosea and Amos began their ministry. As the reigns of Jeroboam II and Uzziah move towards their end, a foreign menace begins to loom large. After some centuries of weakness, Assyria was now flexing its muscles. Assyria is mentioned frequently in Hosea, but in Amos, Assyria is a shadowy and threatening presence in the background.[3] Yet clearly judgement at the hands of a foreign power is threatened. The other issue is internal. New wealth had come through control of trade routes and was leading to the emergence of a new upper class with a luxurious and exploitative lifestyle was developing. Some of Amos' most savage indictments are addressed to the complacent rich who oppress the poor (e.g. 2:6-8; 4:1-3; 5:8-13; 8:4-6).

(ii)   Seeing the big picture of salvation history
Amos also places his message in the context of the big picture of salvation history. We see this in his reference to Zion/Jerusalem (v. 2). Both terms refer not only to the literal city but to the people of God in both the Old and New Testament and to the completion of God's purposes in the New Jerusalem. This means first that God's judgement has a precise location; it is not simply a generalised working out of cause and effect. In Amos, and in other prophets, notably Isaiah, Jeremiah, Ezekiel and Malachi, Jerusalem represents the entire community of God's people and the recipient of both judgement and mercy. The name 'Zion' is a very important biblical one; it originally referred to the ridge between the Kidron and Tyropoean Valleys where David's

city was built. Therefore, the reference here in verse 2 is a link with 'David's tent' (9:11) (NIV) and shows the importance of Zion/Jerusalem in Amos' theology. The Psalmist associates it with Yahweh's kingship (e.g. Psalms 47, 48 and 146) and thus it has significance for all time and eternity.

We can see many applications for God's people today. We are not a political state, yet we are 'a holy nation' (1 Peter 2:9). We have both privileges and responsibilities and indeed will not escape judgement if we turn away from God. Thus the specific situation of eighth century BC Jerusalem speaks beyond its time right into ours.

Plainly there is a theology of history here. God is at work now in the ongoing revelation of history, but his ultimate purpose will be realized not in David's city but in the city where David's Greater Son reigns supreme. Our preaching needs to do justice to both emphases. We need to demonstrate how the gospel changes lives and communities in the actual circumstances where people live. Yet we must avoid a 'social' gospel which ignores the eternal nature of Zion/Jerusalem and becomes simply another political and social activity. As evangelicals, we rightly reject such an emphasis, but sometimes it has led to our neglect of human suffering. Amos, properly taught, will send some in the congregation to work in a youth club for disadvantaged youngsters, care for the elderly, visit prisoners and the like. As preachers we need to pray that the living Word will change lives in all kinds of ways.

(2) God is Lord of Creation

The created order, as much as the sweep of history, belongs to the Lord and Amos indicates this in verses 1-2. Again, the reference to the earthquake is significant – a sign that judgement is to come. We need to emphasize that everything, including disasters such as earthquakes, are part of the providence of God. Yet this is a message which is difficult both to preach and to hear. Two things need to be said. The first is that such events are part of God's judgement on a fallen world. We know from Genesis 3:17-18 that Adam's sin resulted in the earth itself being cursed, and from Romans 8:19-22 that when the children of God are finally glorified the creation will be set free from that curse. It is in this context that we must preach the judgements of God in and on a fallen world. Secondly, we have no warrant to say that because particular people are caught up in tragedies, they are especially wicked. Luke 13:1-5 speaks of two such events: a tower falling on some workmen and an atrocity committed by Pilate. The point of these stories, as Jesus makes plain, is that we all stand under God's judgement and thus we all need to repent. Amos is surely making a similar point here.

This intervention of God concerns the whole of creation. A favourite Hebrew way of expressing totality is by pairing opposites, e.g. 'heaven and earth', 'good and evil'. Here the whole of the land and, by implication, the whole world is symbolized by the flat lands where sheep graze and the heights of Carmel. Once again, this is echoed in the last chapter, where the impossibility of escaping God wherever we go, including Carmel, is underlined (9:2-4). The theme is still judgement; the pastures 'dry up' or 'mourn' and the top of Carmel 'withers'. Drought (4:7-8) is one of the signs of God's judgement and shows that he is active in his creation. This emphasis on creation is to run throughout the book.

Preaching and Teaching Notes

As we preach through Amos or teach it in a Bible study context, we will find these three themes of the God who speaks, the Lord of History and the Lord of Creation at the heart of all he says. Some important issues for preaching and teaching Amos emerge from this.

The first is that Amos is a book about God. As we preach it we will be making great affirmations about God and how he relates to this world. Often preaching is ineffective because it is problem-centred and becomes simply good advice or moralizing. Preaching which mediates the presence and power of God will deal with problems far more effectively and will put them in their right perspective. Amos' God is a great God, the God of the cosmos, the God who directs world affairs, a God who is infinitely able to deal with any matter we may bring to him.

Second, the emphasis on judgement will have to be a significant part of our teaching on the book. Prophetic preaching on judgement is in fact the beginning of that judgement, since it calls us to repentance and faith. Such preaching is not comfortable; but it is an integral part of the gospel. Without such preaching people will continue blindly towards that final judgement, seeing no need to repent.

Third, and as already noted, our preaching must rightly tackle the social concerns addressed by Amos. Two errors need to be avoided. The first is to use Amos merely as a vehicle to comment on contemporary social issues. This is to abuse the pulpit because Scripture then simply becomes an adjunct to our own political and social views and we make speeches rather than sermons. The second is to spiritualize Amos' message and ignore the actual poverty, misery and oppression in society. We will guard against both errors if we remember that this is the Word of God which challenges, rebukes and is above any human system. Before we make the necessary applications to our own day we must do responsible work on the text. Accordingly, I will try to give concrete examples when we come to a detailed examination of Amos' social critique.

Fourth, Amos presents his material in striking and unusual ways (we shall find much more of this). He links vision and word and uses evocative terms like 'roars' of Yahweh. As preachers we need to be continually searching for new and imaginative ways to present the life-giving Word. The message is non-negotiable, but we need to stir our hearers out of complacency (see 6:1) and, through mind and imagination, penetrate to their wills.

Fifth, these are not Amos' opinions. They are his 'words', forged in the white heat of revelation and experience and shaped by his own personality, yet they have the authority of the Word of God. Thus, as we have seen, he presents great biblical doctrines, but he does so in his own style and relates them to his own situation. Our preaching needs to follow this pattern and be both predictable and unpredictable; predictable in the sense that it engages with and expounds the great, unchanging biblical doctrines and unpredictable in that it is mediated through a personality and must be personally received and shaped before passing on to others. Totally unpredictable preaching is probably heresy; totally predictable preaching is certainly boring.

In terms of a structure for an opening sermon or Bible study, I would suggest something along the following lines:

Title: 'The Awesome God'
The Lord God of History and Creation speaks

Text: **Amos 1:1-2**

Structure:

1.   **God Speaks**
      (i)   God speaks through his messengers
      (ii)   God speaks in visions and words
      (iii)   God speaks directly into the world

2.   **God is Lord of History**
      (i)   God's particular intervention in salvation history
      (ii)   Seeing the big picture in salvation history

3.   **God is Lord of Creation**

These are great truths to be expounded. However, as suggested in chapter 1, you may want to preach or teach these verses as part of a single sermon or study on chapters 1 and 2. In that case, the essence of verses 1 and 2 would be compressed in a section on the awesomeness of God, with the rest of the sermon or study dealing with the demands of God on the nations (material to be discussed in our next chapter). Whatever way you treat the material, it is important to see that in these introductory verses we have the major themes of Amos set down, which will be amplified through the rest of the prophecy.

Endnotes

1. Alec Motyer has a delightful comment here, Never did a lion make a greater error of judgement (in *The Message of Amos:* The Bible Speaks Today Series (IVP, 1974) p. 27.

2. From the Preface to H. A. L. Fisher, *A History of Europe* (Fontana 2nd edition 1961).

3. Unless 3:9 should read 'Assyria' instead of 'Ashdod', as in some Greek versions of the OT.

3

'CALLING THE NATIONS TO ACCOUNT'

The sweep of God's judgement

(AMOS 1:3–2:16)

Introduction

Amos has clearly set out his themes: the God who speaks, the Lord of History and the Lord of Creation. Fundamentally, he is a God who reveals himself. At this juncture, these themes are set specifically in the context of Amos' time, with the 'Oracles Against the Nations'. We learn how this doctrine of God relates both to the surrounding nations and to the chosen people themselves. At first sight much of this seems unpromising material for preaching, but there is a great deal here that speaks with uncompromising clarity to our day and generation. Two questions arise. What is the overall emphasis of this section? And what can we learn from the careful structure of the oracles?

(1) *Theological emphasis*

First of all, what is the theological emphasis of these oracles? Oracles against the nations appear in many of the other prophets (e.g. Isa. 13–23; Jer. 46–51; Ezek. 25–32;

Obadiah; Nahum; Zephaniah). These passages show that all nations are accountable to Yahweh. This is a development of the theme of Deuteronomy 32:8: 'When the Most High gave to the nations their inheritance'. The moral law is written in all human hearts even if they do not have specific revelation. Conscience dictates that kindness and respect, both for human life and the property of others, are writ large in human legislation, even if they are, in practice, ignored. This material can and ought to be preached. Like Amos, we need to be aware of and articulate about what is happening around us.

This section also gives us biblical authority for mission, a point we need to emphasize clearly in an increasingly multi-cultural world. God is not only Lord of the chosen people, but Lord of all nations and of every human life. Jesus is the only Saviour and his gospel is the only gospel. He will be the Judge of the whole world on the Last Day. It is important to notice that throughout these oracles God himself is the agent who brings about judgement: 'I will break', 'I will strike', 'I will send', etc. are the characteristic expressions. The overall emphasis is that God is at work in history and his hand is present in what we see as secondary causes. These are specific examples of how God is both concerned for and at work among all nations, particularly among his own people.

When preaching on this section we are dealing with the gospel's concern for justice, fairness and humility. This is not a 'social gospel'; rather, it is the social and ethical fruits of the gospel. Amos is exposing the evil and cruelty of the present world which will make the new world of the salvation oracle (9:11-15) all the more striking by contrast.

(2) *Structure of the Oracles*

The first thing which strikes the reader is the four-fold pattern evident in each of the oracles.

1. The origin of the message
2. The comprehensiveness of the message
3. The punishment
4. The concluding emphasis on origin

Each oracle begins and ends with the affirmation that this is the Word of the Lord. What we have, therefore, are specific examples of Amos' general affirmation that God speaks. The repetition of the pattern in each of the oracles is clearly a device to fix the message in his hearer's minds. 'For three sins...even for four' is a Hebrew way of expressing comprehensiveness (similar examples can be found in Prov. 30:15-31). The suggestion is that the whole life of these nations has become corrupt. Amos' oracles have specific and numbered sins in mind, not just general sinfulness.

These sins arise not from negligence or weakness, but rather from deliberate intent. The word used is *'ps'* which means rebellion and wilful breach of trust. The nations are accountable and will pay: 'I will not revoke the punishment' is a repeated refrain (e.g. vv. 3a, 9a, 13a etc.). God has spoken and that Word will carry out its purposes. The oracles then enumerate the specific sins and outlines appropriate punishments. Plainly, there is much here to help us in responsible preaching on God in history; particularly the fact that judgement, while it will finally come on the Last Day, is also evident here and now.

The reason for the order of the nations is not entirely clear. Each one, however, played a part, usually hostile, in the history of Israel and we can imagine the satisfaction with which Amos' listeners would have heard judgement pronounced on every one of them (1:3–2:3). We can also imagine even greater satisfaction as the Lion roars against Judah (2:4-5), their southern neighbour, whom they probably hated even more. And then, of course, we can imagine their utter dismay when the Lion pounced, with the longest and fiercest roar directed against themselves (2:6-16).

This section is probably not best handled by a verse by verse exposition. Many of the themes are repeated and the whole passage has a cumulative effect which needs to be brought out. Dividing the section as follows is helpful:

The Surrounding Nations and the Judgement of God (1:3–2:3)
The Chosen People and the Holiness of God (2:4-16)

This allows us to concentrate separately on the message to the nations and on the message to God's chosen people. Although both are accountable to God, Israel is *especially* accountable (an issue to be taken up in chapter 3 and following).

The Surrounding Nations and the Judgement of God (1:3-2:3)

God's judgement is related to his character and thus is never arbitrary. In these six oracles certain themes are identified as worthy of judgement, evidencing the Lord's concern for basic human rights and standards of behaviour. It would be useful, indeed necessary, to study these verses with a good commentary which will supply important background information (see Appendix: Further Resources for Teaching Amos).

Cruelty and acts of inhumanity are particularly condemned (e.g. 1:3, 6, 11, 13). Vivid imagery is used to suggest ruthlessness and contempt for human life. The indictment against the Ammonites (1:13) is particularly poignant, not only because of the wanton cruelty against pregnant women but also because of the destruction of growing life. There is here, and throughout these oracles, a sense of the value of human life and the anger of God against those who treat it with contempt. Since humanity is in the image of God these acts are rebellion, the punishment for which will be exile and death.

As already noted, ultimately God is the author of exile. Just as Adam and Eve were exiled from Eden and Cain wandered in the land of Nod, so punishment will overtake their descendants. Seven times God says: 'I will send a fire' (1:4, 7, 10, 12, 14; 2:2, 5). At one level this 'simply' refers to burning of cities, but is also a powerful reminder of God's blazing holiness. Indeed, it is a further reminder of the early chapters of Genesis, and the flaming sword which barred the way to the tree of life (Gen. 3:24). Amos is entirely consistent with these earlier Old Testament accounts of sin and judgement. God's fire knows no boundaries; later Amos is to have a vision of this fire devouring sea and land (7:4-6). Likewise, God's judgement on the nation of Egypt involves fire from heaven in the plague of hail and lightning (Exod. 9:13-35). The significance of this is that while Amos is condemning these nations, he is preparing to speak to God's own people, and his indictment of them is to come, not only in terms of universal responsibility, but in terms of the specific responsibility of those who know the Lord.

The Chosen People and the Holiness of God (2:4-16)

As judgement moves on to Judah and Israel, the form of the indictment remains, but the content changes. The specific sins in both Judah and Israel are related to their failure to live in the light God has given. At first sight, the offences may seem minor compared to those of the surrounding nations, but in reality Amos is exposing the underlying causes for their sinful behaviour. Five main issues are identified as the root of the sinful condition of God's people.

(1) Rejection of God's Law (2:4a)

Rejection of God's Law heads the list. From this, all other sins flow. This is Amos' basic conviction; that hearing the voice of the Lord is at the heart of knowing God. It is interesting to note the two terms Amos uses here. 'Law' (or 'Torah') is the whole Word of God, including the words Amos himself is speaking. 'Statutes' (or 'decrees') are the specific commands addressing particular situations. In our preaching we need to keep both aspects firmly in mind. In particular, we need to be aware of the place of Amos (or any biblical book) in the canon as a whole, and grasp its overall theological message. Not only are God's people subject to the same moral code as the other nations, they have been given the Word of God, especially that Word given through the medium of Moses and the Prophets.

(2) Idolatry (2:4b)

Idolatry is closely linked with rejecting the Word. We have already seen in 1:1-2 how the Word and vision go together. Rejecting the Word of God opens the door to a world of fantasy and unreality. The issue in focus here is succinctly captured in these words attributed to G. K. Chesterton: 'When men stop believing in God, they don't believe in nothing. They believe in anything.'[1]

Amos is introducing here what is a common prophetic theme (e.g. Isa. 2:20; Jer. 50:2; Hab. 2:18). Rejecting the worldview embodied in the Torah led to a lifestyle of unreality (examples will be given in the oracle against Israel and are more fully developed in the rest of the book). That idolatry will be consumed by the fire of Yahweh. This was to be fulfilled when Nebuchadnezzar's armies destroyed Jerusalem. The post-exilic prophets, Haggai, Zechariah and Malachi, condemn much in the life of the people, but not idolatry; the exile had burned that out of them.

(3)   Oppression and sacrilege (2:6-8)

Oppression and sacrilege are the substance of the first part of the oracle against Israel. Two points need to be made. The first is that Amos' hearers in Bethel had probably enjoyed the condemnation of Judah even more than that of the other nations. 'Judah' and 'Israel' here are geographical terms, but in the rest of the book 'Israel' is to be used for the whole people of God. Secondly, although the Torah is not mentioned again at this point, the indictment against Judah for rejecting God's Word is plainly also addressed to Israel.

The major theme is oppression and the abuse of power, closely linked to the themes of rejection of the Torah and idolatry. The Torah speaks of a God who is all powerful and before whom we are creatures without independent resources. Without revelation, that is a truth which we learn reluctantly and easily forget. At its root, idolatry is self-love. In such circumstances, we end up enthroning ourselves, with the inevitable consequence of contempt and cruelty towards others.

This contempt for others expresses itself in the treatment of people as economic commodities: '...they sell the righteous for silver, and the needy for a pair of sandals' (2:6b). This violates the Torah's regulations for compassionate treatment of the poor (Exod. 22:25-27; Lev. 25:35-38). The result is physical cruelty – 'trampling' (2:7) - and blatant injustice, which in turn results in sexual abuse and sacrilege. In essence, this is a criminal abuse of male and patriarchal authorities which, instead of protecting women, treats them as objects. There is much cause here for sober reflection in our own day on the way the whole glamour industry treats women simply as objects for men's gratification. When we realize that some, at least, of this sexual exploitation happened at shrines, we realize how corrupt Israelite worship had become (see esp. 5:21-27).

(4)   Contempt for their history (2:9-10)

This section reveals that God's people do not care about what he has done for them in the past. The mention of the Amorites reminds us of the promise to Abraham of land (Gen. 15). The mention of this, as well as the Exodus, highlights their debt to the God who worked through Abraham and Moses. Amos is not calling the people to live in the past, but rather, to re-engage with the God who is still active in their present history. Two aspects of God's acts are highlighted: the first is that he destroyed their enemies and he did that thoroughly (2:9); the second is that he rescued them and cared for them. Thus we have the twin themes of judgement and blessing which permeate the book, but also a reminder that God's people are utterly dependant on his protection. The

Amorites were far stronger (2:9) and the desert was a hostile environment (2:10), and yet God kept them safe. Amos is touching on their ingratitude, a matter which will surface again and again throughout his prophecy.

(5)   *Lack of discipline (2:11-12)*

A lack of discipline amongst God's chosen people is shown by their rejection of spiritual leaders. Prophets (and this will become clearer in 3:7-8) are part of God's gracious provision to call his people back to godly and disciplined living. The command not to prophesy is to become deeply personal for Amos in 7:10-17. This strikes a powerful chord in our contemporary world; the attempt to silence the prophetic voice through obsessive political correctness which will not allow sin to be called sin nor permit prophetic words about the uniqueness of Christ. It is salutary to remember that this is not new, rather a contemporary example of a recurring problem. The emphasis here, however, is particularly on the Nazirites. The laws governing their lifestyle can be found in Numbers 6:1-21 with the emphasis on abstinence from alcohol and the requirement for ceremonial cleanliness. The people deliberately tried to corrupt those who displayed a disciplined and godly lifestyle.

Announcement of judgement (2:13-16)

Having identified the sinfulness of God's people, the inevitable announcement of judgement comes. Moreover, as the analysis of Israel's sins was the longest, so this judgement oracle is the longest. God had once destroyed the Amorites (2:13); now he is to destroy the Israelites. The imagery of the cart is striking and unusual, and not altogether easy to interpret. Possibly the best way to understand it is to think of the overloaded cart splitting open the earth. In that case, we have another reference to the earthquake (1:1; 8:8; 9:1-4) and another echo especially of the opening verses where Amos sets down his major themes. Verses 14 and 15 show the futility of human power against God (a striking contrast to Isaiah 40:28-31 where God's power sustained human weakness).

The chapter concludes with the affirmation that this is the Word of the Lord (2:16b) and the certainty that judgement will come. For Israel and Judah this has the special emphasis that their whole history had been shaped by God's Word and their whole sense of identity as a nation was intimately related to that. The theme of accountability runs throughout and is related to the degree of enlightenment people have. In the case of Israel and Judah it is not simply common morality but the Torah which is the standard by which they will be judged. This is the bridge into the main section of the book, where the focus will be on the chosen people and their responsibility. They stand guilty of the same sins as the surrounding nations but are without excuse.

Preaching and Teaching Notes

In preaching or teaching a section like this we need to be careful to see where the prophet's priorities lie. Two things can be said. The first is that the repeated, 'Thus says the Lord', shows the importance of the material; it is not simply social and political commentary. As in the letters to the seven churches (Rev. 2-3) it is the divine comment on the reality of what is happening. All 'prophetic' preaching needs to bring the Word of God to bear on the situation and to get underneath the surface. We are shown what angers God, and we can be certain that this is still the case. It is especially important that when we preach on national, social and political issues we are not swayed by partisan considerations.

The second significant factor is the implied contrast between general and special revelation. All nations have some revelation of God's 'eternal power and divine nature' (Romans 1:20), which means they must answer to him. However, special revelation comes in the Torah as well as through the prophets to Israel, which means that they know exactly what God requires. It is important for preachers to grasp this distinction and to expound it. On the one hand it means that the voice of God can be heard in any human heart and, on the other, that the voice of conscience and common decency cannot in themselves save; for that we need the living Word of God.

In terms of a structure for a sermon or study, I would suggest something along the following lines:

Title: **'Calling the Nations to Account'**
The sweep of God's judgement

Text: **Amos 1:3-2:16**

Structure:

1. **Introduction to the Oracles**
    (i)   Theological emphasis: surrounding nations/general revelation; chosen people/special revelation
    (ii) Structure of the oracles

2. **The Surrounding Nations and the Judgement of God** (*1:3-2:3*)

3. **The Chosen People and the Holiness of God** (*2:4-16*)
    Basis of indictment:
    (i)   Rejection of God's Law (v. 4a)

(ii)   Idolatry (v. 4b)

(iii)   Oppression and Sacrilege (vv. 6-8)

(iv)   Contempt for their History (vv. 9-10)

(v)   Lack of Discipline (vv. 11-12)

Announcement of judgement (vv. 13-16)

Endnotes

1. Contrary to popular belief, it is unlikely that Chesterton wrote or spoke these exact words. That apart, they make the point here very well!

PART TWO:

Indictment and Judgement on Israel

Amos 3:1–6:14

4

'IF GOD IS AGAINST US'

The justness of God's judgement

(AMOS 3:1-15)

Introduction

The section from 3:1-6:14 constitutes a major section of
Amos. The overall theme is indictment and judgement on
Israel. The section comprises five oracles: three announcement oracles, followed by two woe oracles. Four sermons
are suggested for this section, based on the following division of the text: (1) the first announcement oracle (3:1-15);
(2) the second announcement oracle (4:1-13); (3) the third
announcement oracle and first woe oracle taken together
(5:1-27); and (4) the second woe oracle (6:1-14). The next
four chapters take each of these in turn.

All of us have derived great encouragement and comfort
from Romans 8:31: 'If God is for us, who can be against
us?' Amos 3 faces us with the grim mirror image – if God is
against us, who can be for us! The solemn words that begin
this section of Amos summon the people of Israel to hear
the judgement that the Lord has spoken against them (3:1).
It is a section that contains much salutary teaching for the

church on the perils of complacency, arrogance and the gulf that often exists between what we profess and who we are.

In terms of the flow of the text, Amos develops three aspects of God's judgement, each of which is expressed in powerful and emotive language. These are the fairness or equity of God's judgement (vv. 1-2), the inevitability of judgement (vv. 3-8) and the comprehensiveness of judgement (vv. 9-15).

(1) God's Judgement is Fair (3:1-2)

First, Amos reminds his hearers that God's judgement is just. 'Hear this word that the Lord has spoken' (v. 1a) is not simply the introduction but an integral part of the message. This is not simply Amos' own analysis, it is a direct word from God. 'Hear this word' occurs again in 4:1 and 5:1 and such phrases as 'declares the Lord' occur frequently throughout the book. It is probable that we have an echo of the 'Shema', that affirmation at the heart of Israel's faith: 'Hear, O Israel: the Lord our God, the Lord is one' (Deuteronomy 6:4). This conviction that the Lord must be at the centre of their lives and will have no rivals was crucial at the time Amos wrote. It is no less crucial now.

Amos draws deeply on the earlier Scriptures to show how fair and unbiased God's judgement is. 'People of Israel' refers to both kingdoms, the entire 'family' whom God brought up out of Egypt. The Exodus event is central in the Old Testament and it points to that greater Exodus which is to be accomplished by Christ on the cross and vindicated by his resurrection. Indeed, in Luke 9, when Moses and Elijah speak with Jesus that very word is used: '...and spoke about his departure [Exodus], which he was about to accomplish at Jerusalem' (Luke 9:31).

The fairness or justness of God's judgement is embodied in two important words in the text. The first is 'known' (v. 2a) which the NIV renders 'chosen.' 'I have known' means far more than known about; it is a word of relationship, of covenant. Amos never mentions the word 'covenant', yet this is one of the places he uses language associated with it. The most striking use of the word 'know' in the sense of intimate relationship is Genesis 4:1 where it is used of Adam and Eve. What Yahweh is saying here is that Israel is the only nation with whom he is in a covenant relationship. This makes the next word all the more striking: '…therefore I will punish you…' (v. 2b). The word 'punish' can also be translated 'visit'. This word occurs in several significant contexts. In Genesis 50:24-25 Joseph uses this term as he is dying, assuring his family that God will 'visit' them and take them to the promised land; a clear reference to the Exodus. These words are repeated in Exodus 13:9 just as the Israelites leave Egypt. Here in Amos, the word is turned on its head; God is going to reverse the Exodus and send his people into exile. This, of course, does not mean that God reverses his covenant. Rather, it is judgement within the covenant which removes those who claim to belong but do not, and from which the chastened remnant emerges purged and refined. Psalm 89:32 (where the same word 'punish' is used) makes the point clearly: 'I will punish their sin with the rod, their iniquity with flogging; but I will not take my love from him, nor will I ever betray my faithfulness. I will not violate my covenant or alter what my lips have uttered' (Psalm 89:32-34) (NIV).

This exodus/exile polarity lies at the heart of Old Testament history. The expulsion of Adam and Eve from Eden and Cain's wanderings in the land of Nod in exile from

Paradise merge into the story of Abraham leaving the city of the world to travel to the city whose builder and architect is God. Then we find Jacob and his sons back in Egypt and the need for the Exodus itself. Daniel 1:1-2 attributes the exile of Judah into Babylon to God's own intervention: 'In the third year of the reign of Jehoiakim king of Judah, Nebuchadnezzar king of Babylon came to Jerusalem and besieged it. And the Lord gave Jehoiakim king of Judah into his hand...' Isaiah 51:9-11 sees the return from exile as a new Exodus, a passage which also points to that great Exodus accomplished in Christ. Amos is therefore painting on a broad canvas with a few well-chosen strokes. We must continually engage with the big picture and see where the specific text we are studying fits into that larger canvas.

(2) God's Judgement is Inevitable (3:3-8)

Some commentators suggest that 3:1-2 is followed by an indignant protest from a bystander, forcing Amos to justify his authority for speaking as he does (therefore they take vv. 3-8 as a retort). While there is little doubt that Amos would be challenged by such hecklers (indeed, when he is challenged by the king's priest Amaziah in 7:10-17, he specifically replies to the accusations), here we must be wary of reading more into the text than is there. The silence of the text on this issue makes the point, that what is more important is the authority of the message rather than the status of the messenger. The language, vivid, proverbial and pictorial presents us with the inevitability of judgement. Yet, as we shall see, judgement, while inevitable, can be prepared for. Such preparation must lie at the heart of preaching on judgement.

Amos asks a number of rhetorical questions as a way of forcing his hearers to engage with the issues. An important part of preaching is helping people to ask the right questions. Amos is showing how the pattern of event and consequence is a visual demonstration of the truth of which he has spoken. The first of these questions (v. 3) continues the theme of relationship. Plainly it is the relationship of Yahweh and Israel which is intended. The verb is in the imperfect tense, suggesting not just the occasional walk, but an habitual activity. The clear implication is that the initial call of Israel needs to be sustained by continuing to walk with God. It is, however, precisely because that relationship of 'walking with God' has been broken, that the question of the inevitability of judgement is raised.

The illustrations in verses 4 and 5 about a lion's prey and a bird caught in a snare force us to the same conclusion – the hunter will get its quarry. We know well who the lion is from 1:1-2; and we know that by answering 'no' to these questions the hearers are laying themselves open to the full force of Amos' message. Leaving us in no doubt as to the import and clarity of what he is saying, Amos moves from country to city (v. 6) and to a direct reference to Yahweh. Again, Amos gets behind secondary causes and shows that judgement is from God. It is clear now that the judgements spoken of in chapters 1 and 2 are both inescapable and will bear particularly heavily on the chosen people. As preachers it is incumbent upon us to present people (not least in the family of God) with the inescapability of judgement when the covenant is broken.

It is also clear, however (and this is hugely important), that these verses announce salvation. The lion's roar and the trumpet blast are the voice of God calling his people to repentance. The voice of the prophet points to the future in order that people may come to faith in the present. God reveals his plans to the prophets not only as a guarantee of their certainty but as an opportunity for us to make our peace with him before he comes in judgement. The response to this message must be that fear of the Lord which leads to wisdom. Verse 8b is notable in its reiteration of an important point. Amos is reaffirming what he had already stated in 1:1, that the words are his, with all the verbal dexterity, eye for vivid imagery and poetic intensity he can muster! Yet, fundamentally, these are the words of God himself who has chosen Amos to pass on this message. As we preach on Amos (and indeed on any biblical text), although our words are not inspired like those of Amos, we need, by diligent and prayerful preparation, to ensure that what we preach is the living Word of God and not simply our own reflections on the issues of the day or whatever.

(3) God's Judgement is Comprehensive (3:9-15)

Amos now begins to expand on the nature of the judgement. With startling irony he summons the old enemies, the Philistines and the Egyptians, to look in amazement at the sinfulness of God's own people.[1] Samaria was a city of great wealth and had been built by the warlord Omri, Ahab's father (1 Kings 16:24) on a hill three hundred feet above the plain. This was surrounded by higher hills, and Amos imagines these powerful foreigners looking into Samaria from these hills with disgust and disbelief. Israel is condemned not only by the Torah but by standards of international decency. Unrest and oppression encapsulate the sinfulness of Samaria, suggesting a violent and anarchic society where exploitation and contempt for others was the norm.

To illustrate his point, Amos singles out three aspects of Israel's life, communicated in the text through the three sayings beginning respectively, 'Proclaim' (vv. 9-11), 'Thus says the Lord God' (v. 12) and 'Hear' (vv. 13-15). Taken together, they present a comprehensive indictment against God's people.

(i)   *'Proclaim to the strongholds in Ashdod' (3:9-10)*
There is a complete breakdown of good relationships in society (vv. 9-11). The key to such a breakdown is: 'They do not know how to do right' (v. 10a). Normal upright behaviour eludes them, leading to gross materialism and violence in defence of wealth and privilege (v. 10b). This will result in oppression of the oppressors and the destruction of strongholds and fortresses. The impressive façade of strength and wealth built up in the days of Uzziah and Jeroboam II is about to crumble to dust (v. 11). The question of enduring relevance to the church is where do we find our security and in whom do we trust?

(ii)   *'Thus says the Lord God' (3:12)*
Moreover, there is a loss of personal holiness and the consequent sense of priorities. Verse 12 draws a vivid comparison between a few fragments of a lamb rescued from the mouth of a lion and the tiny remnant of Israel which will survive the judgement.[2] The point that Amos is making is profoundly ironic. Whereas, at least the scraps of the lamb are recognisable as lamb, what remains in Israel is now *only* the evidence of luxury, indolence and complacency – 'the corner of a couch and part of a bed' (v. 12b). Only in the extravagant mercy of God is there grace enough to see anything here worth rescuing. The breakdown of society is

simply an outward evidence of the loss of personal holiness
and spirituality; the abandonment of both the communal
and personal walk with God.

(iii)   'Hear, and testify against the house of Jacob' (3:13-15)
But what about the structures of their faith and worship?
Amos now turns to the altars which symbolize corporate
worship and introduces a theme which he will develop more
fully in 5:18-27. External forms of worship are worthless
if personal and corporate holiness are lacking. Verses 13
and 14 are full of reminders of who God's people are and
where they have come from. The phrase 'house of Jacob'
recalls their origins and Jacob's life-changing encounter
with the Lord at Bethel (Gen. 28). Now it is no more than
an idolatrous shrine. It was Jeroboam I, who reigned from
930–909 BC (1 Kings 12:25–14:20) who had sacrificed to
the golden calves at Bethel (1 Kings 12:32). Jeroboam I was
not advocating the worship of a god other than Yahweh,
rather he was trying to reduce the Lord to a local godlet
who could be represented by the bull-calf, the well-known
Canaanite fertility symbol. Such confusion always leads
to moral compromise. Canaanite religion, as we know
it from the Ugaritic texts, placed no emphasis on moral
scruples. There was no decalogue equivalent and no call for
holiness. In Romans 1:18-32, the apostle Paul reveals the
consequences of this kind of religion where 'they exchanged
the truth about God for a lie and worshipped and served
the creature rather than the Creator,...' (Romans 1:25).
    Amos further emphasizes his point by listing the titles of
God to show by contrast what Israel's religion has become.
He is Yahweh, the God of the Exodus, of Sinai, of the
Covenant, who is bound in a marriage relationship to his

people. He is the 'God of Hosts' (v. 13b), the leader of the armies of heaven and the Divine Warrior (Exodus 15:3).[3] This is also to be a feature of the doxologies throughout the book (4:13; 5:8-9; 9:5-6). In naming God, Amos issues a powerful call to take God seriously, to fear him and to love him. To ignore and flout such a God is to forfeit his protection, symbolized by the horns of the altar being cut off (3:14b). The horns were projections from the flat top and were grasped by those seeking refuge. Their bogus religion would prove powerless to save them.

Their magnificent houses would likewise fail to protect them (v. 15). Ahab had a winter palace at Jezreel (1 Kings 21:1) and another at Samaria (1 Kings 21:18), and it may be that Amos is evoking the memory of one of Israel's most wicked kings to make his point yet more strongly. Amos concludes the section, with the emphatic words: '...declares the Lord' (v. 15b).

Preaching and Teaching Notes

Before offering a suggested structure for preaching or teaching this particular chapter, it might be helpful to say something first about preaching on judgement.

Excursus: Preaching on Judgement

This particular section of Amos and, indeed, the majority of the book, consists of judgement oracles and visions. Indeed, judgement is the dominant theme throughout the prophetic literature. What are the implications of this?

First, if we are to preach biblically, we must preach on judgement. This may seem obvious, but while it may be obvious, equally, it is largely unheeded in the churches of our day. We must be prepared to preach God's judgement, not only as a warning to those who have no saving faith in Christ, but also to the church, in light of its backsliding, worldliness and idolatry. God is as inflexible under the new covenant as the old; much is expected of his people in light of the privileges of revelation. If the church loses its distinctiveness as God's new society on earth, it will inevitably come under the judgement of God. Amos 3 verses 7-8 speak of the role of the prophets in the announcing of judgement. We are not prophets, but as we preach their words we need to be faithful in following their example. This is closely related to the life-changing power of the Word and the authenticity of its message. The one thing a false prophet will never do is tell people they need to change!

Second, we must be careful to preach God's judgement and not our own judgementalism. A text frequently quoted is Matthew 7:1: 'Judge not, that you be not judged'. The point is that our knowledge of the situations and motives of others is imperfect, and that we ourselves are accountable before God's perfect knowledge and judgement which exposes everyone and everything in its burning light. This, of course, is no bar to preaching on judgement, but rather a warning to be thoroughly God-centred in our preaching. One certain way to make sermons on judgement seem little more than scolding is to be issue-centred. Amos has plenty to say about particular issues, but these flow from the God he knows and who has called him to speak. He emphasizes the intervention of God in history in the Exodus, his covenant relationship and his holiness, all of which give lasting significance to his words and force us to get ready to meet that God (as he will say directly in 4:12). In addition, references to the lion in Amos 3 (vv. 4, 8 and 12) are a vivid reminder of the power and awesomeness of

God, who alone has the right to speak words of judgement. As we expound God's Word of judgement, our sermons need to allow the God of the Bible to meet with his people, eliciting their worship and adoration, borne of their fear of the Lord. How sharply this exposes the reductionism that views preaching merely as explaining the text.

Third, we must preach judgement soberly. There is a great emphasis on the Word of God in Amos 3 (vv. 1, 10, 11, 12 and 13) as well as the powerful description in verses 7-8 of what the prophetic Word is. Our preaching, by its close engagement with Scripture and a willingness to listen to the voice of God, needs to have something of the directness of Amos. We need to recover faith in the Word itself as life-giving. The mark of all true preaching is that God's voice is heard. Amos delivers his oracles of judgement in arresting and vivid ways. As we faithfully preach this text, we must be careful not to rob it of its direct and compelling tone. Equally, we must preach judgement graciously, as God's gracious warning to us that we are accountable to him. The announcement of judgement is a call to 'flee from the wrath to come' (Matthew 3:7b). If you are walking along the pavement deep in thought and you step out into the road as a bus travels towards you, the person who pulls you roughly out of the way is your friend, not your enemy. The preaching of judgement is a sign that the day of grace continues. This will not last for ever (see Amos 8:8), but while it does, one of its marks will be preaching judgement.

Fourth, preaching judgement must be carefully applied. We have already seen the general judgement of God on the nations of the world (Amos 1:2-2:3). From chapter 2 verse 4, however, judgement is pronounced on the people of God. Here, judgement is related to the Torah, the Exodus and the way in which God has established a covenant relationship with his people. Great privilege leads to great condemnation. Preaching judgement is always aimed at getting past people's comfortable self-deceptions. Many preachers have found that there are those who enjoy hearing judgement preached because it can be applied to someone else. God's Word will always rid us of such false security.

Fifth, and finally, preaching judgement is an effective way of establishing, by contrast, what pleases God. All preaching will be positive in its affirmations of the great truths about the love of God, the wonder of the gospel, the beauty of holiness, the means of grace and the hope of glory. Yet equally there needs to be an exposure of what is wrong and what detracts from the glory of God. It is very easy to live in a muddled and confused state where we fail to see the inconsistency of our own behaviour. Amos will have much to say about this, notably the inconsistency of using the language of worship yet behaving in a way which shows contempt for the Creator who is the Lord of History. A doctor needs to diagnose what is wrong in order to prescribe a cure. Preaching judgement performs that function in relation to our spiritual health.

Suggested preaching/teaching outline

Bearing in mind these points about preaching on judgement, you may want to use the three divisions I suggested earlier in this chapter and preach the sermon on the fairness, the inevitability and the comprehensiveness of judgement. This would be faithful to the text, allowing God's words to speak for themselves, guarding against the various pitfalls identified above. The third section (3:9-15) yields a natural three-fold division. Whereas earlier in this chapter, I used the linguistic markers in the text as sub-headings, I have translated them into more analytical teaching titles, which might be more appropriate for a sermon or teaching outline. I have also included an appropriate sub-division for the central section.

Title: **'If God is Against Us'**
The justness of God's judgement

Text: **Amos 3:1-15**

Structure:

1.   **God's Judgement is Fair** *(vv. 1-2)*

2.   **God's Judgement is Inevitable** *(vv. 3-8)*
     (i)   The lion will have his prey
     (ii) The lion roars for repentance

3.   **God's Judgement is Comprehensive** *(vv. 9-15)*
     (i)   Indictment for the relational breakdown in God's society
     (ii) Indictment for his people's lack of holiness
     (iii) Indictment for his people's abandonment of their spiritual heritage

Endnotes

1. Some Greek versions read 'Assyria' rather than 'Ashdod' (v. 9a), presumably to provide a better parallel with Egypt. However, Amos nowhere else mentions Assyria and it is better to leave the threat unspecified, especially since he has made it abundantly clear that Yahweh himself is the one who punishes.

2. Exodus 22:10-13 speaks of the responsibility of shepherds to salvage such scraps and return them to their owner. Again, the exile/exodus motif is clear.

3. It is a pity that the NIV regularly renders this expression 'Lord (or God) Almighty' rather than the more accurate 'Lord (or God) of hosts'. The phrase conveys God's lordship over the hosts of heaven and embodies the sense of the heavenly hosts worshipping God. This imagery is particularly appropriate for Amos' context, where counterfeit worship on earth is condemned.

5

'PREPARE TO MEET YOUR GOD'

A catalogue of failures

(AMOS 4:1-13)

Introduction

Amos 4:1-13 is part of the major section from 3:1-6:14, where the theme is indictment and judgement on Israel. In this second announcement oracle, Amos amplifies the general indictment of 3:9-15, by specifying a number of areas of failure: failure to care (vv. 1-3); failure to worship (vv. 4-5); failure to remember (vv. 6-11); and failure to engage with God (vv. 12-13). The chapter systematically builds to a climax in verse 12, where Amos issues a direct challenge to his listeners to prepare to meet their God in judgement. The irony is obvious. The fact that Israel has failed to engage with God cannot prevent God engaging with them in judgement. The chapter concludes with the first of Amos' three doxologies (v. 13).

The initial call, 'Hear this word', reinforces Amos' message that the failure to listen to God is the spring from which all other failures flow. It is notable that in verse 2 Amos refers to God swearing 'by his holiness', implying that he swears by his essential nature. Holiness is the quality that makes God 'other' than everything else and causes sinners to tremble (see e.g., Gen. 3:10; Isa. 6:5). That is exactly the response which Amos seeks from his preaching in this chapter (particularly as he exhorts his listeners to prepare for their day of reckoning).

As we work through this section of the text and then through the rest of the prophecy, we should be vigilant to Amos' versatility in employing different literary styles and techniques in order to embody his message as effectively as possible.

(1) Failure to Care (4:1-3)

Amos focuses first on the indulgent rich and their oppression of the poor. This is a society wallowing in self-indulgence. Immediately our attention is gripped by a provocative and stinging phrase: 'Hear this word, you cows of Bashan...' (v. 1a). Bashan was part of Gilead east of the Jordan and proverbial for its fertility and animal husbandry. We would be mistaken to see this as gratuitous rudeness, for Amos is about to demonstrate how all this selfish luxury is built on oppression. Nor are his remarks anti-women (the same condemnation is made of men in 6:1-2).

The verbs used in verse 1 are participles suggesting habitual activity. It is easy to see how indulgence and oppression are two sides of the same coin. If our main concerns are our own comfort and self-importance, then we will soon regard others with contempt. We will create a situation which is utterly self-centred, where there is no pronoun but 'Me', no number but 'One', no job but 'My' job, no church but 'My' church. In such an environment, God's society will rapidly disintegrate into worldliness.

The punishment will be severe. The 'cows' will indeed be treated like animals by their captors and led like a herd through the broken city walls into bitter exile (vv. 2-3). This is the Word of the Creator who has made the universe in such a way that self-seeking and oppressive behaviour will not prosper. 'The Lord God has sworn by his holiness' (v. 2a) – powerful words indeed! It is necessary to see the importance of this in preaching on the passage. Amos' preaching (and indeed ours) is not a rant from an angry and embittered man against the reality of living in a fallen world. Rather, it is a clear statement that the holiness of God has consequences for every area of life.

(2) Failure to Worship (4:4-5)

The focus now switches to the organised religious life of Israel. The biting irony continues as Amos exposes the sham that underlies their religious observances. Amos makes a number of points which are instructive in helping us to preach effectively on spiritual reality (or otherwise) in our worship. Some commentators point out that Amos may be parodying some of the pilgrim songs, 'Go to Bethel', 'Go to Gilgal' (v. 4a). We have already noted the association of Bethel with Jacob's meeting with God (Gen. 28), and Gilgal is associated with the entry to the promised land where Joshua set up twelve stones (Joshua 4:19-20; 5:1-10). The whole activity of 'worship' associated with these shrines has become a mockery. Amos refers to at least three reasons.

First, 'worship' had become an exercise in self-congratulation, with people bragging about their contributions (v. 5). We need to apply this without blunting the point. It is easy to talk of empty religious practice and imply that this is something of which others are guilty. We can distance the impact of this passage by speaking of the corruption and hollowness of late medieval Christendom with its sale of indulgences, the abysmal ignorance of many of the clergy and the empty ritualism. But where does this bite today? The huge emphasis on image and presentation invariably turns into a snare. There is a thin line between presenting our church as attractively as possible, which is good and glorifying to God, and simply indulging in an orgy of self-approbation. Reading advertisements in church newspapers for ministers, it would seem that every church in the land is friendly, supportive and eager to move forward in mission. Why then is contemporary Britain a spiritual wasteland?

Secondly, their 'worship' ignored the Word of God. Notice the little detail in verse 5: 'Burn leavened bread as a thank offering' (NIV). Leviticus 2:11 and 7:11-14 prescribe the use of unleavened bread for thank offerings. Leaven is often used as a symbol in Scripture for something which permeates either positively (as in Matt. 13:33, referring to the growth of the Kingdom of Heaven), or negatively (as in Matt. 16:6, 11, referring to the false teaching of the Pharisees). Here the associations are entirely negative.

Thirdly, their 'worship' had become self-satisfying rather than God-glorifying: 'for so you love to do' (v. 5b). There is no humility, no sense of awe at the presence of God. The entire ritual is an empty and offensive charade. Indeed, their religious practice is not merely compromised; it is rebellious, blatant sin (v. 4). Going through the motions of piety, when the heart is far from God, is deeply offensive to a holy God.

Preaching like this is never going to be popular. And yet we must remember that prophetic preaching shows that God is determined not to leave his people alone. He will continue to reveal himself and thus continue to call his people back to lives of holiness. Both these notes need to sound clearly: God's holiness and God's mercy which longs to embrace us.

(3) Failure to Remember (4:6-11)

In this next section Amos forces his hearers to face up to the reality that God is at work among his people. There are eight references to God in the first person. The first of these in verse 6 is emphatic (the sense is, 'It was I' / 'I was the One'). This divine intervention is starkly contrasted by Israel's intransigence. Five times the phrase, 'yet you did not return to me', hammers home their rebelliousness. Here Amos is using a literary form (often referred to as 'salvation history') whereby he recites particular historical events in Israel's history confirming God's covenant dealings with his people, as a call to faithfulness on the part of his readers in the present. We see this in the Psalms (e.g. 78, 105 and 106). Once again, Amos' arguments are an amplification of the attributes of God described in 1:1-2; a God who is sovereign in his activity as both Lord of Creation and Lord of History.

Israel had failed to learn from her history. Above all she had failed totally to learn that God's sovereignty over nature and the course of human history is absolute. Nothing, not even apparently chance phenomena, such as rain or indiscriminate slaughter in battle are beyond him. No other view of God will do. That is why open theism is a theology which robs us of the gospel.[1] Unless God works everything according to his will, we may ultimately end up on the losing side. Of course, we have responsibility, otherwise why would Amos be castigating us for failing to return to God? But God is sovereign and will do exactly as he promised.

Two matters merit further exploration here. The first is the purpose of judgement. Judgement is in order to turn people back to God. Famine and drought (vv. 6-8) remind the people that they depend on God for the basic necessities of life. The absence of spring rain would destroy the barley in May and the wheat in June. Amos is emphasizing that this was no meteorological freak but the Creator himself calling to his people to turn to him. Blight and mildew added to the misery by destroying the main food crops (v. 9). The fourth and fifth judgements shift from God as Lord of Creation to Lord of History: the fourth is plague associated with battle (v. 10) and the fifth, the overthrowing of cities (v. 11).

The second matter is the emphasis on what Israel has become. She has degenerated to the status of Egypt, the ancient enemy, and Sodom and Gomorrah, proverbial for their wickedness. We cannot but remember our Lord's words as he speaks of communities rejecting the gospel: '...it will be more bearable for the land of Sodom and Gomorrah on the day of judgement than for that town' (Matt. 10:15 also 11:24). What can this mean? What could be worse than gang rape, sexual deviance and cruelty? Surely, the prideful unbelief which boasts of a special relationship with God and yet dishonours his holy Name and flouts his Word.

There is much heart-searching material for preaching here. We must avoid speaking of our nation as 'chosen' in the same sense as Israel was (lest we substitute nationalism for the gospel). And yet, I think, we can legitimately speak of the privileges Britain and the West have enjoyed which render us the more accountable and indictable before God. We have enjoyed centuries of faithful gospel preaching, a flood of Christian literature and a bewildering array of attractively presented Study Bibles. When we add to that the massive Christian contribution to education, health and all aspects of humane civilisation, we thank God. Yet much of this lies discarded and despised amidst a Gadarene rush away from a godly worldview and lifestyle.

Behind all this lies the concept of covenant, although the word is not mentioned. Here is a God committed to his people and in relationship with them. These events of famine, plague and war are related to the curses God said would come if they broke that covenant (see Deut. 28:15–29:28). God wants repentance, not because he enjoys seeing people suffer and grovel, but because he wants the broken relationship restored. He wants the 'burning stick snatched from the fire' (v. 11b (NIV)). Bearing in mind the explicit reference to Sodom and Gomorrah, this may be an implicit allusion to Lot and his daughters being saved from the fiery judgement.

(4) Failure to Engage With God (4:12-13)

In these final two verses in the chapter, Amos' argument reaches its climax as he exposes the failure which lies behind all the others: Israel's failure to engage with God and take him seriously. The irony is strong. Their failure to engage with God will not prevent God engaging with them in judgement. Two literary forms are employed: an appeal (v. 12) followed in verse 13 by the first of the doxologies (see also, 5:8-9; 9:5-6). Structurally, this collocation is very effective. The appeal follows the uncompromising passages we have looked at and shows that this is a God who is determined to meet with his people in judgement. The doxology is a powerful and rich theological reminder of who God is.

The appeal (4:12)

Consider first the appeal to Israel to meet their God. The text presents some difficulties of interpretation, in particular

what 'thus' and 'this' refer to.[2] What God intends is not
specified but it seems reasonable to take 'thus' as referring to
the punishments of verses 6-11 and 'this' to the impending
meeting with God. But what does it mean to 'meet' God?
Some commentators (rightly in my view) point out that
the Sinai event is probably in Amos' mind. In Exodus 19:17
we read: 'Then Moses brought the people out of the camp
to meet with God'. Earlier in the chapter (vv. 11-15) Moses
had instructed the people to prepare themselves in various
ways for that encounter. The actual meeting with God is
accompanied by fire, smoke and thunder (vv. 16-19). Here in
Amos, the lion's roar creates the same sense of awe; plainly this
meeting is going to be one of terror rather than rejoicing. The
description of the Lord coming to his temple in Amos 9:1-10
is terrifying. And yet, there is grace even there. The closing
words of the prophecy, 'your God' (9:15b) make it clear that
the covenant relationship is still intact. This is biblical grace
and there is nothing cheap about it – wrath meets mercy.

The doxology (4:13)

The doxology (v. 13) is an example of true worship as
opposed to the false worship which Amos has denounced.
This is the God whom Israel will meet; not some Baal-like
idol of their own imaginings. Important truths about God
emerge from this which are true both, in general, and flow
particularly from their context in this part of the book.
Even if Amos is using a fragment of a hymn (which is a
reasonable assumption) he has skilfully applied it to his
particular purposes; namely, that God is capable of carrying
out what he says.

God is the Creator, and Amos uses the words 'yatsar'
(to form) and 'bara' (to create) (v. 13a). These are the

principal verbs used in Genesis 2 and Genesis 1. Together, they encapsulate the biblical doctrine of the Creator God. 'Create' (the verb used in Gen. 1) is only ever used of God and speaks of his transcendence, of the God who is greater than and outside of his creation. He speaks and creation springs into being. 'Form' (Gen. 2), is a word used of both God and humans. It is the potter's word. This is the God who comes down into his creation and shapes and moulds it for his purposes. Taken together, they embrace the transcendence and immanence of God.

It is vitally important in our preaching that we emphasize and hold together these two attributes of God. If we emphasize only the transcendence of God, we will inevitably lapse into deism. The God we speak of will indeed be all-powerful and majestic, but such a God will be remote from and indifferent to our prayers and problems. Our experience of him will be formal: reflected in worship which lacks warmth and humanity, detached from the reality of daily experience.

If we emphasize only the immanence of God, our God will be someone we can intimately relate to, but our conception of him will, all too easily, reduce him to a God made in our image. We will have the vulnerable God, beloved of much modern theology, but crucially no certainty that such a God can save us. Rather than worship marked by awe and reverence, it will become overly familiar, casual and sloppy. It is, however, when we embrace transcendence and immanence (as God *and* Scripture intend) that we have a transforming and life-giving God, the God who has revealed himself in the Lord Jesus Christ, who is both one with God and who became one of us – *and still is one of us*. This God is the lion who roars and yet also the shepherd of his people.

Here, in Amos, the reference to God forming the mountains and creating the wind draws attention both to the massive solidity of creation and its dynamism, which reflect a Creator who is both unchanging and yet willing to respond to movement towards him. He is the God of revelation, who 'reveals his thoughts to man' (v. 13). He does not leave us without a word from himself, a truth of revelation that lies at the very heart of Amos' ministry. The references to Genesis 1 and 2 show us that right from the beginning God is speaking and revealing himself.[3]

Moreover, God controls the daily rhythms of light and darkness as well as the inaccessible 'high places' (v. 13).[4] His power is total in heaven and on earth and he is Yahweh of Hosts, whose name, character and power stand behind the prophet's assertions of who he is.

Preaching and Teaching Notes

The four divisions I have suggested would provide an appropriate structure for preaching or teaching this chapter. The final indictment of failure (failure to engage with God (vv. 12-13)) serves as a summary, establishing the root cause of all Israel's failures and functions as a climax to the chapter – prepare to meet your God in judgement.

Title: **'Prepare to Meet Your God'**
A catalogue of failures

Text: **Amos 4:1-13**
Structure:

1.   **Failure to Care** (*vv. 1-3*)

2.   **Failure to Worship** (*vv. 4-5*)

3.   **Failure to Remember** (*vv. 6-11*)

4. Failure to Engage with God *(vv. 12-13)*

    (i)   Appeal: 'prepare to meet your God' (v. 12)

    (ii)   Doxology: the God we will meet (v. 13)

Another way into preaching or teaching this chapter could be turning these negatives into positives and showing how avoidance of these failures is precisely the way in which we can meet with God, engaging with him as his faithful covenant people, rather than meeting him in judgement.

Prepare to meet God:

1. By Being Compassionate *(vv. 1-3)*

2. By Truly Worshipping *(vv. 4-5)*

3. By Learning From History *(vv. 6-11)*

4. By Bowing in Awe Before Him *(vv. 12-13)*

In both suggested outlines the unifying factor is a life which centres on God and engages with him seriously, lest he engage with us in judgement.

Endnotes

1. I commend to you John Frame's, *No Other God: A Response to Open Theism* (P&R Publishing, 2001) as an excellent treatment of this issue.

2. The NIV obscures the meaning by rendering both words as 'this'; the ESV restores the contrast: 'Therefore thus I will do to you, O Israel; because this I will do to you'.

3. The phrase is ambiguous and can mean that God declares to man what his (man's) thoughts are. The reference would then be to God understanding exactly what is in the human mind.

4. The reference to 'high places' here may refer to idolatrous shrines such as those destroyed by the reforming kings Hezekiah and Josiah. Micah 1:3 has a similar reference.

6

'STOP PLAYING AT MEETINGS'

False security in religious practices

(AMOS 5:1-27)

Introduction

Amos 5:1-27 continues the major section from 3:1-6:14, where the theme is indictment and judgement on Israel. The section begins with Amos' third announcement oracle (5:1-17) which takes the form of a lament (this oracle also includes the second of Amos' doxologies (vv. 8-9)). This is followed by the first of Amos' woe oracles (5:18-27). The unifying theme in this chapter (and hence our treatment of the two oracles together) is Israel's false security in its religious practices (a theme Amos will return to in 8:4-6). In one of his sonnets, Shakespeare comments: 'Lilies that fester smell far worse than weeds.'[1] Here, in Amos 5, we surely have an example of festering lilies. Set against the standard of what constitutes true worship of God and the social justice which flows from it, Amos laments over the perversion of Israel's worship; no longer do the words of the Torah and the sense of God's holiness mark the religious gatherings. The people are playing at meetings and this is creating a lifestyle marked by lack of reverence, compassion and a total absence of reality. In the second woe oracle (6:1-14), Amos shifts his focus from Israel's false security in religious practices, to their false security in military success and material possessions (we will deal with this separately in the next chapter).

In terms of the structure, I will say something first about the nature of the oracles Amos uses in chapter 5 of the prophecy and how they constitute a pivotal point in the development of his argument. We will then work through each of the oracles separately, while at the same time keeping in mind the common theme of religious hypocrisy. The chapter concludes with some notes and discussion on preaching this chapter, which is arguably the most complex and dense in the book.

Amos' lament and woe oracles

Taken together, the two literary forms used by Amos here, a lament (vv. 1-17) and woe oracle (vv. 18-27), are a powerful combination and a striking reminder that both are essential elements when preaching on judgement. The lament, addressed to the entire nation, is also used by Jeremiah and Ezekiel, and the book of Lamentations gives an extended example. Two striking features characterize Amos' lament: first, the tenderness and godly compassion of the prophet (Amos longed for the people to repent and took no pleasure in preaching judgement); secondly, the literary form of lament gives a penetrating thrust to his preaching on judgement. Normally such laments would be for the dead or dying and yet here the patient is still *apparently* healthy under the strong rule of Uzziah and Jeroboam II. The woe oracle (vv. 18-27) is the mirror image of the lament.

'Woe' is often associated with lamentations for the dead (e.g., 1 Kings 13:30; Jer. 22:18). To pronounce 'woe' is the opposite of 'bless'. The biblical concept of blessedness is not only an experiential state of deep inward security, but a statement of benediction that speaks of future destiny. The kind of conduct Amos is castigating with his woes will lead to inevitable judgement.

The use of the literary forms of lament and woe signal a clear watershed in the text. As Amos has already announced the death of the nation, a lament is appropriate. Later in the first two visions (7:1-6), he is to show a similar concern for the fate of the nation: still alive, but soon be taken into exile to Assyria. The whole atmosphere has the eeriness of someone reading their own obituary. Repentance is still urged, but a time will come when even that will no longer be available (8:7-9)!

Amos' Lament (5:1-17)

Further evidence that this chapter functions as the heart of Amos' prophecy is seen in the striking chiastic structure of these verses. Following the introductory oracular formula in verse 1 (with its particular reference to lamentation), the chiastic structure can be seen as follows.

    [1]**Lament:** the nation's funeral (vv. 2-3)
      [2]**Appeal:** seek the Lord and live (vv. 4-7)
        [3]**Acid test:** evidence of a people seeking the Lord (vv. 8-13)
      [2]**Appeal:** seek good and live (vv. 14-15)
    [1]**Lament:** the nation's funeral (vv. 16-17)

Lament: the nation's funeral (5:2-3)

Amos is shocking his hearers out of their complacency. He speaks of the death of Israel as a past event.[2] There is a delicate tenderness in the phrase 'the virgin Israel'(v. 2a), which suggests vulnerability and the unrealized potential inherent in her untimely death. The land, long ago promised to Abraham, has become a grave instead of a refuge. This is reinforced by verse 3 which speaks of sweeping destruction (cf. 3:12). It is notable, however, that a remnant is spared.

The section is given added poignancy if there is an allusion here to the shrine at Gilgal (which I think is probable). Gilgal was where the people first camped on entering the promised land under Joshua (Joshua 4:19-20). It was where the covenant was renewed and the people first ate the fruit of the land of Canaan (Joshua 5). It was a base for Joshua's wars of conquest (Joshua 9, 10 and 11). It was at Gilgal that Saul was confirmed in his kingship (1 Sam. 11:14-15). It is also notable that again Amos reminds his hearers that his words are God's words (v. 3a).

Appeal: seek the Lord and live (5:4-7)

Amos is a master of surprise. He has been mourning the death of the nation and yet suddenly he offers life: 'Seek me and live' (vv. 4a, 6a). This phrase embodies both command and promise. There is a further irony. Seeking God does not mean going to the great pilgrim shrines. The prophet is warning against a disastrous misconception of worship, for these very shrines were themselves destined for judgement (v. 5). The 'house of Joseph' will be destroyed by fire (v. 6), which we have already seen as the agent of judgement in the oracles against the nations in chapters 1 and 2 (indeed, we will see it again in 7:4-6). The shrine of Bethel will itself not be saved, nor will it save its adherents.

It has often been felt that verse 7 is misplaced, yet surely it fits here perfectly. While alleging they were seeking God, their relationships were inconsistent with his holiness. The verb translated 'turn' is used in 4:11 of God's overthrow of Sodom and is a reminder of how perverted all their thinking and behaviour had become. We are mindful of Jesus' words in Matthew 7:21-23, as he castigates those who call him Lord and speak and act in his name, yet have no relationship with him.

The fundamental problem is that the people of Israel did not take God seriously. Words such as covenant, justice and righteousness, did not set their hearts on fire. True worship is when God's character shows itself in every aspect of his people's lives.

Acid test: evidence of a people seeking the Lord (5:8-13)

In the second of his doxologies (vv. 8-9), Amos reminds the people who God is and how far they have strayed in their understanding of him and his requirements. They may 'turn justice into bitterness' (v. 7) (NIV), but this God 'turns blackness into dawn' (v. 8) (NIV). The point is that God is sovereign; no power can undo what he decrees. Israel is heading for destruction at the hands of a greater power. The doxology in vv. 8-9 is, then, not simply a splendid hymn of praise to God, but fits the context perfectly, reinforcing many of Amos' themes.

Verse 8 shows the power of the Lord of Creation, and verse 9 the power of the Lord of History, which, as we saw in 1:1-2, are dominant themes of Amos.[3] The reference to the stars in verse 8 echoes Genesis 1:16 – 'He also made the stars' (NIV) – and refers to God's providential control over the seasons (Pleiades and Orion mark the beginning and the end of the sailing season). He also controls day and night and is Lord of the waters (demonstrated both in creation and the flood). This is the mighty God of their Scriptures, the God they claim to worship when, in reality, they are dishonouring his name.

This God is also supreme over human power (v. 9), an idea which has already appeared in chapters 1–2; 3:15; 4:1-3. God has the power to judge the wealthy and strong and will have no truck with arrogance (Amos expands on this theme more fully in chapter 6). The doxology is a powerful demonstration of how worship and godly living cannot be divorced. We live in the twin categories of space and time and are called to praise and serve the One who made both, and who demands that our words of praise be reflected in transformed lives.

If we truly seek God, there will be clear evidence of the fact. We might well refer to this as the 'acid test'. What Amos describes in verses 10-13, however, is not evidence of authenticity, but a marked *lack of evidence*. The first mark of truly seeking God is to love God's Word (v. 10b). In stark contrast, they 'hate' and 'abhor' (v. 10) those who speak the truth with the integrity which God's covenant demands. This is the antithesis of the Psalmist's statement, 'Oh how I love your law' (Ps. 119:97). Their character and lifestyle were contrary to the principles of God's Word, which results in a deliberate and concentrated attempt to overturn justice.

The rejection of truth leads to oppression of the poor – the absence of servant-heartedness or concern for others (v. 11). This will certainly lead to punishment for no one can evade the Lord's all-seeing eye. Sadly there is no place for protest (v. 13) and voices raised will be silenced. Of course the silence does not include Amos, a reminder that it is precisely at times of departure from God that the prophet's voice needs to be heard. Nor is the Lord himself silent. The roar of the lion is heard both in the words of Amos and in the unfolding events.

Appeal: seek good and live (5:14-15)

Having established beyond doubt that the Lord is intending to punish their sin, Amos now returns to appeal (vv. 14-15). God's presence is dependent on his people's obedience. They are to seek good which here is identified with establishing justice. The implication is the creation of a society which will please God when he looks on it. There are overtones of Genesis 1, when God pronounces creation to be good. Amos offers no guarantees. It 'may be' that the Lord will have mercy (v. 15b). He is the Lord of Hosts, neither beholden to anyone or anything, nor owing us any favours. And mercy, if he so chooses, will come 'to the remnant' (v. 15b), not to the whole nation. The reference to 'the remnant' is the only basis for hope and for the continuing of God's purposes.

Lament: the nation's funeral (5:16-17)

In verses 16 and 17, Amos returns to the lament of verses 1-3. Here is a picture of national mourning: both town and country are involved in the recognition that life as they know it has come to an end. And the agent of judgement is God himself, who will pass through his people as he had once passed through Egypt in judgement (Exodus 12:12).

Lying behind these verses is Amos' determination to make the nation think seriously about its fundamental theological beliefs. The twin poles of the character of God and the people's relationship with him were at the heart of these beliefs. They *professed* belief that God was Creator and Saviour. If such a profession has any substance, then there are profound implications for living. It means that human life is a creaturely life, dependent on the gracious provision of the Creator for life and all good things. It means that his people are obliged to respond to him with joyful praise and a willingness to obey his Word. It means that they need his guidance and protection every day of their lives. Moreover, it demands that relationships with others be based on service rather than subjugation. There is much here that cries out to be preached. Both in the world *and the church* there is often hatred of the one who speaks the Word of God and an arrogant dismissal of those perceived to be inferior (along with a cringing servility to those perceived to be superior). What is needed is an urgent and thorough return to preaching the gospel of grace with all its implications for living godly lives. God's favour cannot be bought by magic or bribery. Grace is the driving force of the whole of life. Once the link is broken between God's grace and the life which flows from it, false religion takes its place. To place any confidence in such religious practice is false security, and thus there is an urgent need for repentance.

Woe Oracle (5:18-27)

Amos' first woe oracle continues this theme of placing false security in religious practices. No amount of false religion will merit favour with God. Rather, it will merit *and bring* his judgement. A three-fold structure is evident in this oracle: the Day of the Lord (vv. 18-20), God's assessment of their religious practices (vv. 21-24) and a concluding pronouncement of judgement at the hands of Assyria (vv. 25-27). We will consider each briefly in turn.

(1) *The Day of the Lord (5:18-20)*

Amos' use of the term 'day of the Lord'(v. 18a) is rich in irony. One might assume that such a day would be a time of rejoicing for God's people, a time when Israel's enemies will be defeated as in the 'day of Midian' (Isa. 9:4). Surely it would be reminiscent of God's victory at the Exodus (see again Exod. 15:3, 'The Lord is a man of war'; when victories for God's people were secured notwithstanding their failure to live as God's covenant community). Such events were not merely past history. They were kept in the public consciousness by being celebrated, for example, in Psalms such as 136, with its glorious rehearsal of the mighty acts of the Lord in creation and history. And yet when that day comes, says Amos, it will be marked by darkness. This darkness clearly symbolises danger, as the little vignette of the lion, the bear and the snake illustrates (v. 19) (see also Isa. 13:6-16, Joel 2:1-2, 30-31 and Zeph. 1:7-16 where these dark images are developed further). At the Exodus the pillar of cloud as well as the three day plague of darkness had shown the awesome power of Yahweh; now that same darkness would be directed against the Israelites.

Preaching on this needs careful and pointed application. Like Israel, the church today (not least in Britain) needs to face up to reality. It is all too easy to make unbalanced statements about desiring a meeting with the Lord, about being on the brink of revival, without that radical commitment to repentance which, as Amos reminds us, lies at the heart of any true engagement with God. This distorted picture is apparent in an overtly triumphalist tone in many of the worship songs and hymns on revival. People need to know what they are singing when they call for the day of the Lord, or the pouring out of the Spirit of the Lord. We must be clear that the pattern of exile before exodus is a hard, hard road, and yet necessary for the church's restoration. Our task is to preach the Word, believing in its power, and pray to the Lord of the Harvest. Like Amos, we need to call people to repentance and faith, not look to some glory days in the past nor pine for their return.

(2)   *God hates your festivals (5:21-24)*

Here we need to be careful to grasp the sequence of Amos' thought. In all probability, such false notions of the Day of the Lord found expression in the religious feasts and other services. Amos strikes right at the heart of Israel's bogus religion. The absence of the usual, 'Hear this word' or, 'says the Lord', shows that Yahweh himself is speaking, thus adding a particular poignancy and weight to these words. The expressions 'hate', 'despise' and 'take no delight' (v. 21) reverse all that they imagined God thought about their worship. God's *intense* displeasure is made abundantly clear, in that he enumerates the various components of their services and denounces them one by one. This is a comprehensive indictment.

The structure of these verses is clear. In verses 21-23 we have the denunciation of all that is wrong with their worship, and in verse 24, the expectation of what results from true worship, which is so utterly lacking in the life and witness of God's people. The 'feasts' (v. 21a) would include the Passover Feast and Feast of Unleavened Bread, as well as the Feast of Weeks (or Harvest) and the Feast of Tabernacles (or Booths) (see Exod. 23:14-18; Lev. 23:4-44 and Deut. 16:10-16). The reference to 'assemblies' (v. 21b) may have been the climax of the Feast of Unleavened Bread (see Deut. 16:8) or a more general allusion to festival days. The important thing to remember is that these were divinely appointed and remained so during the Old Testament period. When we are preaching on this passage we are not dealing with the kind of service that is essentially wrong, such as multi-faith worship which mentions Buddha and the Hindu writings on the same level as the Lord Jesus Christ and the Bible. That is indeed wrong and needs to be condemned, but it is not the issue here. The issue is the unworthy participation in what is God-given. This is similar to eating the bread and drinking the cup in an unworthy manner (1 Cor. 11:27).

The Lord's general displeasure is directed specifically at the sacrifices offered. The three types of sacrifice represent different elements in worship: the burnt offering wholly given to God (cf. Romans 12:1); the grain offering giving back to God part of his gracious gift in creation; and the peace offering symbolising fellowship with God and each other. Yet because they had comprehensively rejected God their Creator and Saviour, who desired them to have a loving relationship with him and with each other, going through the correct motions was worse than a sham – it was an abhorrent offence. A similar condemnation is directed against their praise. Singing good and beautiful words, without an obedient heart and a willingness to confess sin and be changed, is rank hypocrisy.

True worship issues in transformative action. Verse 24 cuts like a scalpel, contrasting what is expected with the reality in Israel. The stream of righteous living that flows from genuine worship is not to be sporadic, like the water which disappears in the dry season, but a great river of God's justice and righteousness flowing from a truly worshipping people to irrigate the world. Those who praise Yahweh's covenant love must themselves become channels of that grace to those who are thirsty. Such active consequence of faith is wholly absent amongst God's people.

(3)   *Assyrian religion will take you to Assyria (5:25-27)*

This powerful chapter ends with the announcement that exile will be the inevitable consequence of bogus religion. A glance at the commentaries will show that there are a number of difficulties of interpretation in this section. We can, however, see a logical development of thought if we realize that Amos is both concluding this section on false religion and pointing on to chapter 6, which picks up on the foreign threat to Israel (to which they are, at the moment, smugly indifferent).

Amos first addresses the issue of the place of sacrifices by a rhetorical question in verse 25, alluding to that defining event when God gave the law to Moses at Sinai, which indeed included the sacrificial regulations but placed them in the context of love and obedience. We might paraphrase the verse: 'Were sacrifices and offerings all that you brought to me, during the forty years in the desert, O house of Israel?' Without that covenant relationship the whole sacrificial system was simply reduced to playing at meetings. Indeed, it is similar to the passage in Micah 6 which speaks of 'doing justice, loving kindness and walking humbly with your God' as being more acceptable than 'thousands of rams with ten thousands of rivers of oil' (Micah 6:7). The same principle applies to us. We may hear the Word read and preached on, sing fine hymns and speak eloquent prayers, but if our hearts are far from God we are speaking and acting without integrity.

There is a close connection between verses 25 and 26. Verse 25 speaks of ritualistic scrupulousness while the obedience of the heart is lacking. Verse 26 speaks of the same ritualistic adherence to false religious observances. Comparing, for example, the ESV and NIV, we find that the precise meaning of the artefacts of the idolatrous worship is not totally clear. What is clear, however, is that worship of pagan gods, probably with astrological characteristics, is the issue. Alec Motyer comments helpfully: 'The gods of Assyria occupied the hearts of Israel long before the armies of Assyria occupied its streets and towns.'[4] If we are obsessed with externals, then the object and the content of our worship become less and less important. We see this when ministers sit light to the truths of the gospel but rigidly insist on the 'correct' clerical dress or the correct stance at communion. Nor is this confined to one type of church. Whenever our devotion to a way of doing things, whether traditional or contemporary, becomes more important to us than the glory of God and the good of those gathered, then we have lost the very heart of the gospel. Ultimately, true worship embodies a profound simplicity and integrity and touches the whole of life, so that what we say and sing with our lips, we believe in our hearts, and what we believe in our hearts, we carry out in our lives.

All of this leads to the inevitable conclusion in verse 27: Assyrian religion will take you to Assyria. In 2 Kings 17:22-23 we read: 'The people of Israel walked in all the sins that Jeroboam did. They did not depart from them, until the Lord removed Israel out of his sight, as he had spoken by all his servants the prophets. So Israel was exiled from their own land to Assyria until this day.' Amos underlines this inevitable conclusion with a reminder that the word comes from 'the Lord, whose name is the God of hosts' (v. 27b).

Preaching and Teaching Notes

This is a rich and powerful chapter employing many devices and techniques to hammer home the message. While there are two distinct themes, the true worship of God and the justice which flows from it, these are so intertwined that it would be a mistake to try to unpick them for preaching purposes. Indeed it is just this marriage of the two which gives the chapter its power and shows how one cannot properly flourish without the other. Plainly, the heart of Amos' message is the failure to meet God and the lack of a true relationship with him. There are a number of ways in which this material could be profitably structured for a sermon or Bible study. Reflecting our confidence in Amos' logical development of his material, we might profitably use the following structure. Such an exposition will allow us to hold 'appeal' *and* 'lament' side by side, thus adding a weight and poignancy to both.

Title: 'Stop Playing at Meetings'
False security in religious practices

Text: **Amos 5:1-27**
Structure:
1. **Lamentable Worship** (*vv. 1-17*)
    (i)   The 'acid test': evidence of authentic worship (vv. 8-13)
           A people seeking God
           A people serving others
    (ii)   **Appeal:** seek God and seek good (vv. 4-7, 14-15)
    (iii) **Lament:** the time to seek is over (vv. 2-3; 16-17)

2. **False Security** (*vv. 18-27*)
    (i)   What will the Day of the Lord be like? (vv. 18-20)
    (ii)   What does God really think about our wor-

ship? (vv. 21-24)

(iii) What is the consequence of failing the 'acid test'? (*vv. 25-27*)

A number of other approaches would be effective. One would be to take the shrines in verse 5, Bethel, Gilgal and Beersheba, and structure the exposition around the understanding that Amos is addressing the devotees of each sanctuary in turn. This is the approach taken by Alec Motyer and is a fruitful way to tackle the chapter.[5] Another way would be to take the passage on the Day of the Lord (vv. 18-20) as the basis for expounding the rest of the chapter (or the lens through which we might view the chapter). Such an approach might suggest the following structure.

Title: 'Are You Really Prepared for the Day of the Lord?'

Text: **Amos 5:1-27**

Structure:

1. **The Day of the Lord** *will expose who and what you are: (true or false worshippers).*

2. **The Day of the Lord** *will expose what your relationships are like: (serving others or self-serving).*

3. **The Day of the Lord** *will bring irreversible judgement*

Equally, we might take the doxology of verses 8-9 as the key or lens to the rest of the chapter, with a title such as '**What God Demands**'.

1. **God is Lord of Creation** *so must be truly worshipped*

2. **God is Lord of Judgement** *so must be honoured by justice on earth*

3. **God is Lord of History** *so must be trusted and obeyed*

These last two suggestions would involve a more thematic study of the chapter. The important principle in expounding this chapter is to emphasize how the souring of the relationship with God inevitably sours all other relationships.

Endnotes

1. Sonnet XCIV.

2. 'Fallen' (v. 2) is what is known as a proleptic or prophetic perfect, i.e. action is seen as completed.

3. By changing some of the words in verse 9, some commentators find references to stars other than Pleiades and Orion, and therefore take verses 8 and 9 to refer to control over the seasons. We are on much safer ground leaving the text as it is, with references to both creation and history (as in 1:1-2).

4. Motyer, The Message of Amos, p. 136

5. Motyer, The Message of Amos, pp. 105-137.

7

'STOP BEING COMPLACENT'

False security in military success and material possessions

(AMOS 6:1-14)

Introduction

Complacency and apathy are a deadly combination for both communities and individuals, even when grosser sins are absent. The point is made powerfully in Revelation 3:14-22 in the judgement on the church at Laodicea. It is seen no less powerfully here in Amos chapter 6. The unifying theme in this chapter is Israel's false security in military success and material possessions. There is, therefore, a close connection with the previous chapter where false security in religious practices was exposed ('Stop Playing at Meetings'). The root cause of this complacent attitude is the same; a people who had fallen out of a right relationship with the Lord. The God 'worshipped' at Bethel, Gilgal and Beersheba was not the Sovereign Lord of Creation and History, but a godlet, whose purpose was seen to gratify the people's whims, encouraging them in their lives of apathy, luxury and self-indulgence.

Amos 6 concludes the major section of the prophecy from 3:1–6:14, a comprehensive message of judgement presented in a series of five oracles: three announcement oracles and two woe oracles. It is important to see the connection between 5:18 and 6:1. Both begin woe oracles which intensify in menace (see 5:27; 6:7, 14). Amos sharpens his words to show the gravity of the situation (literally the people are 'playing on the brink of the abyss'), and thus builds to his climactic declaration of the coming judgement in the form of a terrifying invader (6:14).

Amos 6 can be usefully divided into two parts: the woe oracle proper (vv. 1-7) and the announcement of judgement (vv. 8-14). There is, however, a clear unity of theme, and the pivotal verse 8 reminds us forcibly of the nature of the God they so take for granted (v. 8 can be considered as a parallel to the doxology in Amos 5:8-9).

Playing on the Brink of the Abyss (6:1-7)

This oracle is addressed to both parts of the kingdom, echoing the end of section 2 (ch. 2:4-16) where both Israel and Judah are denounced (a reminder that Amos' prophecy is directed against the whole people of God). In terms of literary structure, verse 1a embodies a perfect balance between Zion and Samaria ('those who are at ease' and 'those who feel secure'). Again, as so often with the prophets, the main attack is directed against the leaders (v. 1b). They are the ones who are most guilty of being 'at ease'. The verses which follow expose the root and manifestation of this complacency.

False security in military success (6:1-2)
The complacency referred to in verse 1 (the people are 'at ease in Zion') is, in part, a reference to the feelings of

triumph induced by the military successes of Jeroboam II and Uzziah (see 2 Kings 14:23-25; 2 Chron. 26:6-8) (the point is echoed in Amos 6:13). This had led to a complacent sense of security, and, in particular, a blindness to the increasing military threat posed by Assyria. Verse 2 is puzzling and the subject of a good deal of spilt ink in the commentaries! It may be best understood as an echo of the words of the leadership's spin doctors in their propaganda of military success and security. It is also possible that Amos is reminding God's people that since they are indeed *chosen* people ('the first of the nations' (v. 1b)), comparing themselves with other nations in matters of security is, in fact, a sign of weakness. 'Are you better than these kingdoms?' (v. 2b) No, but you should be! 'Or, is their territory greater than your territory?' (v. 2b). No, but it should be!

Our concern here, however, is not with the debates on interpretation, but how best we might apply the thrust of the text. The root problem exposed is a failure to see others clearly because we are blinded by a sense of our own superiority. Secure borders and affluence (at least for some) in Amos' day had induced this sense of security, blinding people to the lessons of history past and present. In the affluent West today, we too are in danger of succumbing to such a failure. We all too easily fall into the mindset illustrated by 'The Guide to Good Churches'. In a major broadsheet newspaper, churches, like hotels, are awarded stars and judged by everything except that one, crucial thing which cannot be judged by us, the condition of people's hearts before the Lord. Just as true faith and worship strive for that integrity where all of life is worship lived in the presence of the Lord, so false faith and worship leads to the opposite, where everything is secularised. We are so easily seduced by our own relative 'success' into imagining God must be rather pleased with us.

Again Amos gives us helpful pointers as preachers in this vital matter of application. We all know how easy it is to say true things which, nevertheless, miss the mark because they are overly vague and generalized. People too easily switch off when complacency or apathy are mentioned because they can so readily apply it to someone else and because, often, they think that their presence proves that they are neither complacent nor apathetic. Amos exposes what complacency truly is and gives specific and pointed illustrations.

Failure to realize there is a Day of Judgement (6:3)
The 'day of disaster' is probably the Day of the Lord (5:18-20). By ignoring the judgement to come they are in fact bringing nearer a reign of terror. In the short term this will refer to the five kings who followed Jeroboam II in Israel in quick succession, some of whom seized the throne violently (see 2 Kings 15-17). When the preaching of a Day of Judgement ceases then complacency reigns supreme.

False security in material possessions (6:4-7)
The picture here is of an extravagant feast. As in Shakespeare's *Hamlet*, where the court of Claudius caroused and revelled while Fortinbras of Norway marshalled his armies on the borders, so here God's people wine and dine oblivious to the reality of the threat of exile. Amos exposes a complacent, indulgent lifestyle (particularly among the leadership). For the average Israelite, meat was an expensive and rare luxury, but here the rich seem to be indulging in several of the more succulent and expensive cuts (v. 4b). Even more striking is the ironic reference to David. How they need a champion

like David to defend the land against dangerous enemies; instead they imagine, because they sing songs, that they have become like the great king (v. 5). The words of Romans 16:18 are applicable: '[They] do not serve our Lord Christ, but their own appetites'. So obsessed have they become with their own luxurious lifestyle that they 'are not grieved over the ruin of Joseph!' (v. 6b). So blinded are they by their own prosperity that they do not see that the nation is doomed (v. 7). Once again, inherent in their complacency is a blindness; there is no sense that one day the party will end. Instead of being at the head of 'the first of the nations' (v. 1b), they would be heading the line trudging off to dreary exile. Their whole self-serving indulgent lifestyle is about to vanish.

Complacency, as exposed by Amos, is no mere feeling; it goes right to the roots of fundamental attitudes and lifestyles. Many of the Psalms (e.g. Psalm 1) speak of that happiness, security and prosperity which spring from obedience to the Torah and the way of life which flows from it. Once again, their failure is that they were out of touch with the living God and thus the source of true happiness and fulfilment had dried up.

Announcement of Judgement (6:8-14)

The final passage in this section of Amos is an announcement of judgement, which also provides a bridge into the major section that follows containing Amos' visions. There is a striking contrast between the luxury of verses 4-6 and the overwhelming devastation of this section.

Divine oath of judgement (6:8)

God commits his full authority (he swears by himself) to carrying out judgement on his disobedient people. Judgement is demanded by the nature of the God who speaks. He is the Lord Yahweh, the God of holiness, redemption and judgement who has saved his people and will now punish them (see 3:1-2). He is the Lord of Hosts whose armies will punish Israel (cf. Joel 2:11 where the invading locusts are identified as the Lord's army). The reason for this judgement is pride; that arrogant and idolatrous self-satisfaction which has been already exposed, and which is symbolized by the fortresses which seem unconquerable but will surely perish (v. 8b). This is bleakly illustrated in Lamentations 2:7: 'The Lord… has delivered into the hand of the enemy the walls of her palaces.'

A picture of the coming devastation (6:9-10)

Amos has vividly painted the decadent luxury; now he portrays the devastation with equal potency. Verses 9-10 balance verses 4-6 and, while the exact meaning of every word is not entirely clear, we can readily grasp the general picture. Whole households are to be wiped out with no mercy shown to any survivors (v. 9). The suggestion is that this is a large family home belonging to rich people. There is an eerie stillness and the sense of a vanished and vanquished community. The charge to 'silence!' (v. 9b) may have a deeper significance than being silent in the presence of the dead. The word translated 'silence' occurs in other contexts of judgement (e.g. 8:3; Hab. 2:20; Zeph. 1:7; Zech. 2:13) and carries with it the idea of silence in the awesome presence of God as he comes to judge.

Invasion is imminent (6:11-14)

It was clear from the 'Oracles Against the Nations' (chs. 1–2) that, whoever or whatever may have been the secondary agents, the Lord himself is the one who judges. And so it is here (v. 11); God himself will fulfil the oath spoken in verse 8 and illustrated in verses 9-10. The phrase 'given the command' (v. 11a) sounds militaristic and is probably a further indication that God the Warrior of the Exodus has turned against his people. Houses, large and small, will be obliterated (v. 11b). The use of words such as 'smash' (NIV) reminds us of the earthquake imagery which is evident throughout the prophecy (1:1; 2:13; 8:8; 9:1-6).

In verses 12-13 Amos uses a style reminiscent of Wisdom literature and, reiterating his own earlier use of rhetorical questions (3:3-8), poses questions which are clearly absurd. Horses and oxen simply do not behave in that unnatural way, yet Israel has behaved in a way that is even more unnatural (v. 12a). Justice has been poisonous instead of life-giving, and righteousness, which should taste sweet and succulent like a fruit, has the bitter taste of wormwood (v. 12b). To use a New Testament parallel, they are manifesting the works of the flesh rather than the fruit of the Spirit (Gal. 5).

There is another absurdity in verse 13 where Israel is boasting of two recent victories of Jeroboam II. The very names of the captured cities reveal the hollowness of the boasts. Lo-Debar is in the Gilead area of Transjordan and Karnaim slightly further north. The meaning of Lo-Debar is 'nothing', which is exactly what had been achieved through this conquest. The meaning of Karnaim is 'double-horned'; 'horn' implies strength and is an ironic allusion to the people's arrogant trust in their own sense of security. Their success was utterly hollow. Again, the complacency theme is strongly underlined.

Verse 14 is the final blow; God's act of judgement, now inevitable, becomes more specific. Assyria is not mentioned, but the invasion will be by a terrifying enemy who will oppress all the way from north to south. For all their boasting, complacency and fancied strength, the people of God can do nothing to save themselves, for Yahweh of Hosts has turned against them.

A Summary of Amos 3:1-6:14

As we draw the threads together, it is helpful to set down a number of markers, which not only summarise this particular chapter, but also allow us to pause and get our bearings as we come to the end of the major section of Amos from 3:1-6:14. The dominant note of these chapters (and indeed the first six chapters of Amos) has been the indictment and denouncement of the sins of God's people. From now on the emphasis will be almost entirely on judgement.

(1) *The root failure is ignorance of the true God*

The point made in verse 8 in this chapter is 'classic' Amos, as he identifies great and eternal truths about God which bear on the present situation. Right from the beginning of his prophecy, Amos has introduced us to an awesome God, sovereign in creation and history and active in both. God's people, however, have put him in a religious box to be 'worshipped' at Gilgal. Amos reminds them here that Yahweh is the universal Sovereign, the Warrior God, and that having forfeited the security offered to those who trust in him, they have no security left. Their God will be wholly consistent with his character and will not tolerate arrogance from Israel any more than from anyone else. We need to realize that God has not changed and that our security, including the future of our churches, depend totally on his help. We have to abandon our faith in secondary means and trust in him alone.

(2) There is a lack of belief in judgement

There was no longer a sense of accountability to God; hedonism and carelessness had become the driving forces in their lives. Verse 6 in this chapter speaks of their failure to grieve 'over the ruin of Joseph', because they imagined that Joseph was in need of nothing. The use of the woe oracle (both here and in chapter 5) is a sign of the seriousness and inevitability of judgement. It shows that Amos is giving a word from God and not simply looking at the national and world scene, thereby deducing what is likely to happen. Judgement is a reality, and to ignore or exclude it from our mindset, is simply to live in a fantasy world.

(3) There are false kinds of security

In this chapter, Amos exposes two areas of false security: first, military strength (the military successes alluded to in v. 2, the fortresses of v. 8, and the meaningless consequences reported in vv. 12-13); and second, a luxurious lifestyle (vv. 4-7). The one dupes them with its appearance of strength, and the other lulls them into a dream-like idyll. In the Western world we are all too familiar with these kinds of security and often we rely on our insurance policies, bank accounts, homes and jobs. The fatal point is reached, when instead of gratefully receiving these as gifts from God, we regard them as our natural rights and build our lives on them. In chapter 5, the false security exposed was empty religion. Playing at meetings is meaningless unless the heart is engaged in worship.

(4)   *Complacency is a serious sin*

Amos' strong words make it clear that complacent apathy is not a harmless, if undesirable, attitude of mind, but a deadly sin which will choke our spiritual life. There is always a danger as time passes for churches and individuals to become 'at ease in Zion' (v. 1a). Many a student of church history has attempted to answer the question: 'Constantine's legalizing of Christianity did more damage to the church than persecution. Discuss.' You get the point! Too many church websites and other publicity material leave an uneasy feeling that we are offering ourselves rather than Christ. Much of the rhetoric that surrounds our evangelism gives the impression that Christianity is a lifestyle option rather than an urgent necessity. Commitment to church attendance is patchy, attendance at prayer meetings for the minority. There is a complacent attitude to the moral state of our society and the importance of Christian distinctiveness within it.

All this makes for uncomfortable reading and preaching. We must remember two things. The first is that God's Word is living and will bring about change in hearts and lives open to him. The second is that here, as always, we are preaching first to ourselves and exposing the dangers of complacency in our own hearts. We preach what we have known and experienced of God's cleansing in our own lives rather than sermonize to others.

Preaching and Teaching Notes

Given the close thematic and structural unity between Amos 5 and 6 (in that both are concerned to expose the complacency that arises from false or misplaced security), a similar structure is suggested here for tackling chapter 6 in a sermon or Bible study. With regard to the issue of false security in military success, the discussion earlier in this chapter indicates how we might best apply that in our preaching.

Title: **'Stop Being Complacent'**
False security in military success and material possessions

Text: **Amos 6:1-14**
Structure:
1.   **Complacency Exposed** *(vv. 1-7)*
      (i)   False security in military success *(vv. 1-2, 8, 12-13)*
      (ii)   False security in material possessions *(vv. 4-7)*
      ...leads to blindness to the reality of coming judgement (v. 3)
2.   **Judgement on Complacency** *(vv. 8-14)*
      (i)   God's divine oath of judgement *(v. 8)*
      (ii)   A picture of coming devastation *(vv. 9-10)*
      (iii)   Invasion is imminent *(vv. 11-14)*

A number of other approaches would be effective. One would be to preach a sermon under the general heading **'Stop Being Complacent'** along the following lines.

Structure:
1.   **Stop Being Complacent** *because God is real (v. 8a)*
2.   **Stop Being Complacent** *because you are relying on false security (vv. 1-6, 8b, 12-13)*
3.   **Stop Being Complacent** *because judgement is coming (vv. 7, 9-14)*

Also, as I suggested in the introductory comments on planning a preaching series, if time is limited, you might want to preach on chapters 5 and 6 together, under a title such as **'Playing with Fire'.**

1. Playing With Fire: *False Security in Religion*
2. Playing With Fire: *False Security in Military and Material Security*
3. Playing With Fire: *The Dangers of Complacency*

Equally, we might turn these negatives into positives, with a title such as 'What God Expects'.

1. God Expects Genuine Worship
2. God Expects Justice and Righteousness to Flow From His People
3. God Expects No Complacency

These last two suggestions would involve a more thematic study of the chapter.

PART THREE:

Visions of Judgement and Hope For Israel

Aᴍᴏꜱ 7:1–9:15

8

'Seeing It As It Is'

Who pulls the strings and who speaks the truth?
(Amos 7:1-17)

Introduction

'Humankind cannot bear very much reality'[1] said T. S. Eliot, and yet it is with reality that the prophet and the preacher continually need to confront people, however unpalatable. In this third and final part of his prophecy, Amos continues in his systematic unmasking of complacency and indictment of the complacent. Whereas, previously, Amos has spoken principally in oracles of judgement, in this section his focus is visions of judgement and their implications for opening eyes to the truth. The activity of God is revealed both in everyday events and cosmic phenomena, with the emphasis on his absolute sovereignty. The mystery of God's ways, both in judgement and mercy, are powerfully presented.

It will be helpful at this point to say something by way of introduction about the structure of the section as a whole, the rationale for dividing the section into manageable units for preaching, and the relationship of word and vision with its implications for preaching.

(1)   Overall structure of section

Amos reports five visions of judgement. The visions carry on the basic themes of the book established in 1:1-2 with an emphasis on God as a God who speaks, revealing his will, and the Lord of History and Lord of Creation. They begin with a glimpse of the process of creation (7:1-3) and end with the destruction of the temple and its inescapable consequences throughout the entire cosmos (9:1-4). Throughout the visions there is a blend of the local and the cosmic. The first four visions include a dialogue between God and Amos, but in the fifth the prophet is merely a spectator who recounts what he sees.

It is possible that the visions follow a temporal sequence. The locusts hatch in the spring and then follow the fires of a dry summer, the fruit harvest in late summer and the autumn festival at Bethel. But more significant is the progress towards judgement; at first Yahweh relents but then proceeds to inevitable judgement.

The first three visions (the locusts (7:1-3), the fire (7:4-6) and the plumb line (7:7-9)) can be considered as a unit. They are followed by Amos' encounter with Amaziah, the priest of Bethel (the King's priest) (7:10-17). This narrative insertion serves to illustrate the consequence of Amos' reporting of the visions (and indeed the consequence of his ministry in general). Amaziah stands opposed to Amos' message and ministry. Amos responds by affirming his call from the Lord to prophesy. The question implied by the text is who speaks the truth, Amaziah or Amos? The fourth vision, the basket of ripe fruit (8:1-3), is followed by a judgement oracle (8:4-14). Structurally, this oracle functions in a similar way to the narrative that follows the first three visions. The oracles elaborate on the implications of the vision. The fifth and final vision and announcement of Israel's destruction (9:1-10) is of Yahweh standing by the altar at Bethel. This is a climactic vision of utter destruction. Embedded within this vision is Amos' third and final doxology (9:5-6).

(2)   *Dividing the material for preaching*

In terms of dividing up the material for preaching, my suggestion is to run with the chapter divisions in Amos, which offer an appropriate thematic as well as structural coherence. The final vision and announcement of destruction, which accounts for the first half of Amos 9, I would suggest should be preached as part of a sermon which takes the entire final chapter of the prophecy. An appropriate title might be 'In Anger Remembering Mercy', embracing the dual themes of judgement and mercy (or exile and exodus). For the remainder of this chapter we will consider in detail Amos 7. In the two chapters that follow we will consider Amos 8 and Amos 9, respectively.

(3)   *Relationship of word and vision*

Before we turn to the meat of the visions, a few comments about the relationship of word and vision will be helpful. We need to understand the purpose and nature of the visions in light of the opening words of the prophecy: 'The words of Amos … which he saw' (1:1). The view of some commentators that Amos is here recounting a series of dreams or ecstatic experiences is wide of the mark. Amos understood clearly what he saw and presents the revelation in vivid language. This is of great encouragement to the preacher, to trust in the power of the spoken word, and to be cautious when listening to those who argue that in our visual culture, drama, visual aids and non-verbal methods, such as mime, would be more effective ways of conveying the gospel.

At the outset, it is important to realize what vision is. Vision is not seeing what is not there; rather, vision is seeing everything that is there. Moreover, vision is given by God and not invented or dreamt up by humans: 'This is what the Lord God *showed me*' (7:1,4,7; 8:1). This divine revelation contained both images and words and the words are essential to convey the message. What is important is that we do not confuse appeal to the imagination with non-verbal means of communication. We have already noted the vivid and colourful nature of the language and imagery of Amos and argued that, as preachers, we need to strive to be as imaginative and pointed as possible in our own use of language, for we convey the revelation not by drawing pictures or using mime but in words. Even when these methods are used they need words to unfold their meaning. The sacrificial system of ancient Israel, the food laws and the like, can be described as 'visual aids', illustrating for God's people God's holiness and their sinfulness. Similarly, baptism and the Lord's supper can be seen as 'acted parables' of God's grace in Jesus Christ – and our response. However, without the Word of the gospel these can easily degenerate into superstitious rituals. With that in mind we now turn to the visions themselves.

The Three Visions: Who Pulls the Strings? (7:1-9)

Vision 1: the locusts (7:1-3)
God at work in creation
In the first vision, Amos is showing Yahweh in the process of forming a locust swarm just at the time when growth

is taking place in late March/April.[2] God is active in the 'normal' processes of the created order and makes use of them to carry out his purposes.

The plague is a devastating one and the whole countryside is stripped bare before Amos' eyes. Two points of note. The first is that there is no mention of Israel's sin, yet the mere fact of a locust invasion is a sign of God's judgement. Egypt had once suffered from such a judgement (Exod. 10:1-20) and plainly Israel is now suffering a similar fate. This is the judgement of the Lord, not a natural disaster, and explains why Amos begs forgiveness (v. 2a).

Secondly, Amos here intercedes as a covenant mediator, recalling Moses' intercession after the golden calf episode (Exod. 32:11-14). What is fascinating is the ground of Amos' appeal: 'How can Jacob stand? He is so small!' (v. 2b). This is particularly poignant considering the earlier condemnation of Israel's boasting about her military strength and invulnerability (6:2, 8, 12-13). We have noticed, especially in the 'Oracles Against the Nations' that, whatever the human or other instrument, it is God himself who is the judge.

The Lord's response (v. 3) emphasizes his sovereign freedom and compassion. For God to 'repent' or 'relent' does not imply inconsistency on his part, but rather a willingness to express his mercy and be faithful to his covenant. This is a principle which runs through Scripture. For example, God was willing to spare Sodom if only a few sinners repented (Gen. 18:22-23). Likewise, he restrained the angel of destruction from sending the plague on Jerusalem (2 Sam. 24:15-16). We dare not presume, however; the judgement is deferred but not annulled.

Vision 2: the fire (7:4-6)
God and the cosmos

The second vision, which also relates to creation, is on a grander scale with overt supernatural elements. The 'great deep' (v. 4b), whether it applies, as some commentators believe, to subterranean waters which nurture growth and would replenish the crops after the locust and fire devastation, or to the deep as home of spiritual forces of evil, clearly has elements of mystery. The judgement of Yahweh will destroy not only human life but also supernatural enemies. The overwhelming wrath of God destroying the whole created order is seen in 2 Peter 3:10 and Revelation 20:11 and is a timely reminder that the whole of creation is in the hand of the Lord. No power in heaven, earth or hell can stand against him. The 'land' (literally 'the portion' (v. 4b)) most probably refers not to the earth in general, but to the land of Israel in particular.

Amos again intercedes, this time using 'cease' rather than 'forgive' which marks a further stage of simply casting himself on the mercy of God (v. 5). He is not even asking forgiveness – simply that God will have compassion. Again God responds in grace and shows his patience (v. 6).

Both visions have shown God's sovereignty in creation and his freedom to act in and through the created order; both his judgement and mercy have been shown to be real. Amos demonstrates how deeply he has absorbed the message by underlining judgement in his report on the visions, and by embodying God's own compassion in his plea for mercy.

Vision 3: The plumb line (7:7-9)
God in history

The third vision deals with earthly, indeed earthy, realities: bricks, walls and a plumb line. We are dealing with the reality of Israel's life from the divine standpoint. Simply looking at a wall will not show if it is built straight, but a plumb line will soon reveal its soundness or lack of it. The spiritual plumb line is the Torah which embodies God's self-revelation and covenant with his people and against that standard they have been found wanting. The phrase 'my people' (v. 8b) emphasizes that they will be judged by covenant standards, a principle we have already seen in 2:4-16. This is reinforced by verse 8b: 'I will spare them no longer' (NIV) or, more literally, 'I will never again pass by them'. The Lord had passed by them in Exodus 12 and destroyed their enemies, but now, by their wilful rebellion, they had angered him to the point that he will not pass them by.

God's judgement here is further defined as an attack on the two institutions at the heart of Israel's national pride and complacency: the religious shrines and the royal house. Both these institutions ought to have modelled how covenant grace operated among God's people. Instead they had become embodiments of self-will, pride, self-indulgence and complacency, all the things which Amos has so clearly exposed in chapters 3-6. The shrines are characterized as 'the high places' (v. 9a). These were sometimes natural heights, sometimes raised platforms, and are regularly condemned throughout 1 and 2 Kings as places of idolatry and bogus worship. Notably, the faithful king Hezekiah is condemned for getting rid of them (2 Kings 18:4). The error here is as old as the tower of Babel; the notion that we get closer to

God if we climb steps and erect buildings which reach up to heaven. The sanctuaries will be destroyed and the military and political exploits of Jeroboam II will amount to nothing but his own destruction, because he has been faithless to the Lord (see 2 Kings 14:24).

In this vision there is neither plea for mercy nor stay of execution. The time for judgement has come and the point of no return has been reached.

Amos and Amaziah: Who Speaks the Truth? (7:10-17)

The dialogue between Amos and Amaziah is instructive on a number of counts. As already noted, it is placed strategically after the three visions of judgement and serves to illustrate the consequence of Amos' ministry. The third vision, followed by the blunt prediction of verse 9, had probably stung Amaziah into action. Amaziah's hostility makes it clear that in no sense is Amos' denunciation of Israel's bogus worship and social injustice overdone. Amaziah is the evidence that it is not! The priest of Bethel is exposed as a self-seeking, unscrupulous politician who will not listen to the Word of God. The plumb line, already applied to religious and civic institutions, is applied to an individual and the result is the same – Amaziah will suffer God's judgement.

Amaziah's protest (7:10-13)

Amaziah's criticisms of Amos' preaching are timeless. The first is that he attempts to represent it as a personal conspiracy against Jeroboam II (vv. 10-11). Amos was not guilty of any attempted coup against the king, nor had he predicted Jeroboam's violent death. Personalizing a general word is a common tactic of those who wish to discredit it. Like all such accusations, it is a mixture of truth and error. It is true that Amos had predicted the downfall of Jeroboam's house and the exile of the kingdom. What is not true is that this is some kind of personal vendetta on the part of Amos. The 'I' of verse 9, the one who will rise up against the house of Jeroboam, is the Lord himself. Amos is the messenger who brings the Word; it does not originate with him. The Amaziahs of this world will consistently refuse to acknowledge that. They will attack the messenger rather than the divine source of the message.

The second objection of Amaziah is that 'the land is not able to bear all his words' (v. 10b). Once again, there is truth in these words; the land is unable to hear Yahweh's words without experiencing judgement. But again Amaziah is trying to relativize Amos' words and portray them as mere demagoguery which is not conducive to the public good.

What makes Amaziah's words so damaging is that they speak in the rather sneering and dismissive tone of the liberal establishment rather than the threatening tones of the persecutor. Many who have stood up to bullies have succumbed to subtle undermining tactics: see the way Hezekiah stood up to Sennacherib in 2 Kings 18 and 19 and yet was seduced by Merodach-baladan in 2 Kings 20. In the West this is our great temptation. We don't like being sneered at and called fundamentalists, and there is a real temptation to tone down our message. We have seen how the message of Amos was misrepresented and a totally false impression given of the man and his motives. This is no less true in our day.

There are other agendas or strategies behind Amaziah's words in verse 12. He attempts to localize Amos' preaching and thus rob it of universal significance. Judah is the right place for Amos to exercise his ministry because they would love to hear denunciations of Israel there. This is another great temptation for the preacher – to denounce what he knows his hearers want to be denounced rather than bring what needs to be heard. It is not altogether easy to read the tone of Amaziah's comments here. The word 'seer' (v. 12a) is not necessarily derogatory and indeed can be considered totally appropriate in this context of visions. It may be that Amaziah is seeking to persuade Amos with a combination of flattery as well as criticism. Alec Motyer points out that 'eat bread there' (v. 12b) is an appeal to job security and an attempt to buy off Amos.[3] In summary, Amaziah employs devious and underhanded approaches in order to save face and avoid unpleasant circumstances.

Verse 13 pictures Amaziah clothing himself in the pomp and circumstance of the establishment. Bethel is the apex of civic religion and subject to the power of the state. This is a royal chapel and one of the great sanctuaries which must have appropriate liturgy, vestments and all the paraphernalia of the church establishment. In such an environment, rather rude prophetic voices are out of place (v. 13). How hard indeed it is for the establishment to hear a prophetic word!

Verses 10-13 show us the outward evidence of what Amos has seen in vision, the clash between two centres of authority. Who speaks the truth? Amaziah or Amos? (or more accurately, God through his prophet Amos). The next section answers the question.

Amos' call (7:14-15)
Many of the prophetic books contain a 'call narrative' (e.g. Isa. 6, Jer. 1 and Ezek. 1; also the call of Samuel (1 Sam. 3)

and the call of Moses (Exod. 3)). Such narratives serve
to authenticate the prophetic word and speak of a direct
encounter with God. Here we have, in brief, an account of
Amos' call and it serves to underline the divine nature of his
mission. This is the fundamental point of the section and we
must not allow controversy over the precise interpretation
of verse 14 to obscure the point. However, we do need to
look carefully at what Amos is claiming.

Amos is claiming authority on a number of grounds.
The first is that of call. If Yahweh had called him then who
is Amaziah to reject him? Amos has been given a word from
God and told to go and tell it. It is in that context we must try
to understand the difficulty of reconciling verses 14-15. The
commentaries have much to say on these verses, but essentially
the problem is that there are no verbs in verse 14, which reads
literally: 'Not a prophet I nor a prophet's son, but a herdsman
and dresser of sycamore figs'. Both the NIV and ESV supply
past tenses, i.e. 'I was not a prophet once (but I am now)'. This
would remove the problem of the apparent contradiction
with verse 15 where Amos says that Yahweh called him to
prophesy. However, if the verbs are present tense, Amos could
be replying to Amaziah that he is indeed prophesying, but is
not a 'professional' prophet 'in it for the money'! This would
emphasize the important point that it is prophecy and not the
prophet, the message and not the messenger, the sermon and
not the preacher which is vital. In either case, the emphasis
is firmly on the authority of the Word of God and not the
personality of the speaker. As preachers, the Word must be
our source of authority. We need to unleash the living Word,
believing in its power to do its work.

We will often encounter people like Amaziah in our
own preaching ministry. We will be told that preaching is

an outdated, élitist and unproductive activity. We need, in these circumstances, to be certain of our call to preach and revisit those moments when we became conscious of that call. We must not allow 'Amaziah' to browbeat us or try to cajole and bully us into setting aside our God-given ministry.

Judgement on Amaziah (7:16-17)

Amos follows his call account by emphasizing that the word he speaks now is the Word of the Lord (v. 16a) and that it is a judgement oracle. The important thing to notice here is the reason Amos gives for the judgement on Amaziah: 'You say,"Do not prophesy against Israel, and do not preach against the house of Isaac"' (v. 16b). It is a serious sin to try to prevent the Word of God being spoken and those who try to do so will themselves be silenced. Ultimately this is where we all stand or fall. The word translated 'preach' suggests a flow of words, possibly indicating contempt (the New English Bible paraphrases 'go drivelling on'), which reflects Amaziah's patronizing disdain for Amos' words.

The fate of Amaziah is a terrible one involving not only him but his family (v. 17). Everything he trusts in will go: he will no longer be able to carry out his priestly role, the nation itself will be rejected and the prophetic Word fulfilled. None of this was inevitable but Amaziah had made his choice, and the Word he rejected became his judge. This will happen when we preach: some will be attracted by the fragrance of Christ and will be saved; others will smell the stench of death and will reject the Word (see 2 Cor. 3:14-17). Each time we preach the Word, the issues are no less than life and death.

Word and vision are inextricably linked in this chapter. The prophetic Word has interpreted the visions and opened eyes to reality. Those, like Amaziah, who refuse to face reality are destroyed by the very Word that they despise.

Preaching and Teaching Notes

The structure of the chapter suggests a clear structure for a sermon or Bible study. The overarching theme is seeing things as they really are. It is our responsibility as preachers to be faithful in expounding God's Word so that eyes will be opened to reality. The bridge between the first and second points of the sermon is, in itself, a clear application (i.e. the kind of preaching that Amos delivers will bring a hostile reaction).

Title: **'Seeing It as It Is'**
Who pulls the strings and who speaks the truth?

Text: **Amos 7:1-17**
Structure:

1.   **Where the Real Action Is – Who Pulls the Strings?** (*vv. 1-9*)

      (i)   The locusts: God is at work in creation (*vv. 1-3*)

      (ii)   The fire: God and the cosmos (*vv. 4-6*)

      (iii) The plumb line: God in history (*vv. 7-9*)

2.   **Where the Real Authority Is – Who Speaks the Truth?** (*vv. 10-17*)

      (i)   Amaziah's prosecution of Amos (*vv. 10-13*)

      (ii)   Amos' defence (*vv. 14-15*)

      (iii) God's prosecution and judgement on Amaziah (*vv. 16-17*)

Endnotes
1. Four Quartets, Burnt Norton Pt 1.
2. The verb is a participle indicating an action already in process.
3. Motyer, *The Message of Amos*, p.171.

9

'A Famine of the Word of God'

The inevitable consequence of judgement

(Amos 8:1-14)

Introduction

Amos 8 continues the major section from 7:1-9:15, where Amos reports a number of visions of judgement on Israel. When we reach this point in Amos' prophecy we face a particular dilemma. We have already looked at the difficulties of preaching judgement (see in particular the excursus on preaching judgement in ch. 4) but here we find an additional problem. One of the reasons for preaching judgement is to shock people into taking action, plead for mercy and amend their lives. But now no such action is possible; judgement is coming and it is inevitable.

Two things need to be said. The first is that a chapter such as Amos 8 is a warning against what Bonhoeffer called 'cheap grace'. The grace of God does not mean that we keep on sinning and then repent and go on to do the same things all over again. Given the nature of God, such an attitude shows that we do not in fact understand his grace. Grace, according to Titus, 'trains us to renounce ungodliness and worldly passions,' (Titus 2:12), and to wait for the day when Christ appears. Once again, the Day of the Lord features prominently in this chapter (vv. 2, 9, 11) and its judgements are certain.

Secondly, we need to be able to recognize the marks of a community which has passed the point of no return. A key phrase is 'the pride of Jacob' (v. 7) by which Yahweh has sworn. Yahweh normally swears by himself or his holiness (see 4:2; 6:8). Here the pride of Jacob has become such an immovable and unchangeable feature of the nation that it can only be dealt with by judgement. This is 'the sin that leads to death' (1 John 5:16), that persistent refusal to listen to God which becomes an inability to hear his voice any longer. It is both the cause *and* consequence of the 'famine of hearing the words of the Lord' (v. 11) which is the inevitable consequence of judgement. Continual rejection of the Word leads to withdrawal of the Word. We need to recognize this terrible arrogance and learn positively how to avoid it.

The structure of the chapter is similar to the previous one: the reporting of a vision (vv. 1-3) followed by an elaboration on the message of the vision (here in the form of a judgement oracle (vv. 4-14)). The opening vision is linked to the encounter with Amaziah (7:10-17) which had illustrated perfectly the pride of Jacob and shown why judgement was necessary. The vision is stark in its impact and all-embracing in its compass – 'my people Israel' (v. 2b). Equally, the announcement of judgement is comprehensive, reflecting many of the themes of earlier passages: cosmic disturbance, empty formal religion, social injustice and exile. As noted above, the chapter builds to its powerful conclusion, a famine of the Word of God.

Vision 4: The Basket of Ripe Fruit (8:1-3)

Israel is ripe for judgement

These verses describe the vision of the basket of summer fruit (vv. 1-2) and give a glimpse of what the judgement will be like (v. 3). The wordplay on 'qayis' (summer fruit) and 'qes' (end) underlines the inevitability of what is to happen. It is difficult to render this wordplay in English although the NIV translation: "'A basket of ripe fruit,' I answered. Then the Lord said to me, "The time is ripe for my people Israel.'" is a good attempt. The basket of summer fruit would be particularly associated with the Feast of Booths (Deut. 16:13ff.) which celebrated the goodness of God throughout the year and looked to future blessings. But this time there was no future. Nature itself was testifying against them. Jeremiah similarly laments: 'The harvest is past, the summer is ended, and we are not saved' (Jer. 8:20). The God of creation is revealing through natural processes that their time is up!

Verse 3 shows what the judgement will be like. It will be drastic; death instead of life. Thus, starkly, the overall message of the Bible is presented: mercy and grace are offered but if these are rejected, there remains only death and judgement. We are reminded again of Amos' deep roots in the earlier Scriptures and the Moses-like nature of his task. Moses says: 'I have set before you life and death, blessing and curse. Therefore choose life' (Deut. 30:19). The people had chosen death and the evidence for that will soon surround them. Indeed the Assyrian exile will be a preview of the Last Day itself.

Judgement Oracle (8:4-14)
A famine of the Word of God

False religion and injustice (8:4-6)

The judgement oracle 'Hear this' (v.4a) begins with an indictment against Israel's false and empty religion and the social injustice (rather than justice) that results. All of this stems from a failure to recognize who God is. Their false views of God had corrupted everything. Amos presents a chilling parody of life lived in the presence of God. When God is at the centre of life, everything else – relationships, work and leisure – fit into their proper places. Here, self is at the centre and proves to be a jealous master, pushing everything else out to the margins. Israel's worship has become boring because, compelled (at least outwardly) to focus on something other than themselves, the people are disengaged. They wish the service would end so that they can get back to the real world. Greed, gain and commerce are enthroned; righteousness, peace and justice are shown the door.

This leads to dishonesty and oppression (vv. 4-5). Their standards were wholly corrupt. They sold small measures of wheat for grossly inflated prices and ruined struggling buyers. It is easy to see how idolatry and social injustice belong together. If ultimately we worship ourselves, and idol worship is a form of self-worship projecting and absolutizing our fantasies and fears on the screen of the universe, we will judge everything and everyone by how they serve our interests. In verse 6 'the poor' are treated as disposable items (commodities to be bought and sold.) What a grotesque perversion of the heart of their faith! Yahweh looked on them as they groaned under the oppressor (Exod. 2:23-25) and came down to rescue them (Exod. 3:8). Truly to believe in a God like that leads to lives of compassion and love, elements conspicuously lacking here. James writes in the spirit of Amos when he speaks of visiting widows and orphans as being at the heart of true religion (James 1:27) and condemns the discrimination against the poor man who comes into the assembly (James 2:3).

Once again, we need to think carefully how to apply this in our preaching. It would be tempting, perhaps, to distance ourselves from the passage. We may minister, for example, in places where there are no wealthy people in our congregations or where the wealthy are models of godly living. But we must not evade the real thrust of the passage which is about self-centredness; this applies across the board whether we are rich or poor. When God becomes simply one of our interests he will soon become irrelevant, diminished and boring because we have ceased to honour him and tremble at his Word. In such circumstances we may be present when the Word of God is spoken, but we will not hear it.

God's judgement (8:7-10)

Amos now sets these actions and attitudes in the context of God's judgement. God swears by 'the pride of Jacob' (v. 7a), which has become such a fixed and immutable attitude, that God's people can no longer plead for mercy. The words: 'Surely I will never forget any of their deeds' (v. 7b) are the very heart of what judgement is about. We are accountable to God who will not ignore or gloss over our infringements of his Word.

This is underlined by another reference to God's judgement in creation (v. 8) which, like the vision of the summer fruit, reminds us that everything in the created order carries out the Creator's will. It is another 'Psalm-like' passage and reintroduces the theme of judgement by earthquake. The Nile has its own particular associations, especially with the Exodus story and the judgements unleashed on Egypt; here (as seen in 3:1-2) that same judgement is to be unleashed on the chosen people. Jeremiah also speaks of the rising of the Nile as a picture of judgement (Jer. 46:7-8). Like the Flood itself God's judgement will cover the whole land.

The judgement continues in verses 9-10 with a solar eclipse. The phrase 'on that day' shows that the prophet is thinking of the Day of Yahweh which would be foreshadowed by the fall of Israel. The atmosphere of revelry (4:1; 6:4-6) will be replaced by that of funeral wake. Once more, as in the judgements on the nations in chapters 1 and 2, God himself is the agent of destruction: 'I will make'; 'I will turn'; 'I will bring' (vv. 9-10). Yahweh is Lord of Creation and History and they will know it. They have failed to 'know' their God with the result that their whole identity and their place in the order of things has become totally confused.

The culmination of God's judgement: a famine of the Word (8:11-14)

The oracle of judgement reaches its climax in the stark conclusion that rejection of the Word will result in withdrawal of the Word. The absence of a Word from God is lamented elsewhere in Scripture. The Psalmist laments: 'We do not see our signs; there is no longer any prophet, and there is none among us who knows how long' (Ps. 74:9). Lamentations 2:9 mourns the fact that 'her prophets find no vision from the Lord'. The 'silence' of v. 3 is that worst kind of silence – there is no Word from the

Lord. But this has been no arbitrary withdrawal; in 2:12 Israel has commanded the prophets not to prophesy and in 7:12-13 Amaziah had reiterated this to Amos himself. Those who continually reject the Word cannot expect that it will always be available.

Amos now spells out what the famine will mean. It will result in a frantic and fruitless quest because, having lost contact with God, the people do not know where to begin looking for him (v. 12). The next tragic consequence is the loss of young life: the cream of the population, beautiful and healthy, will fall fainting (v. 13). With their enthusiasm for living and their readiness to listen to new things the young are always vulnerable to the peddlers of lies. When the Word of God is not heard, the young will feel a need to find refreshment elsewhere and a whole generation will be lost. Earlier generations have a heavy responsibility for exhausting biblical capital and providing only fantasies in its place.

There is a further lapse into idolatry (v. 14). Swearing an oath by Yahweh or some other god was an act of worship and a belief in the authority of the god so named. The text is obscure, but the general meaning of turning to false religions is not in doubt. The 'guilt' of Samaria could, with minor emendation, refer to the goddess Ashimah or Asherah, the fertility goddess, whose prophets had been denounced by Elijah (1 Kings 18:19). The city of Dan was on the northern border of Israel (Joshua 19:47) and there Jeroboam I had placed one of the golden calves (1 Kings 12:29). It is more than probable that such corrupt worship had continued at Dan and led to the kind of situation described by Amos. The third phrase, 'As the Way of Beersheba lives' (v. 14b) is slightly obscure and may refer to a kind of pilgrimage to Beersheba. What is plain is that the corruption had contaminated the whole land ('Dan to Beersheba', like 'Land's End to John o' Groats' means the entire country). Although geographically idolatry is universal, it is particularly concentrated in the capital city with all its influence and prestige.

It is worth reflecting a little more on the famine of the Word of God and how Amos' message applies today. This may be a famine in the sense that it is difficult to find churches where the Word of God is preached in all its fullness. That was the situation in many parts of this country in the first part of the twentieth century. Liberalism had captured the theological faculties and the preaching that results (or lack of it) began to empty the churches. There were churches which remained faithful to the gospel, but often preaching was text-based or devotional; expository preaching where the Bible was unfolded book by book and its message applied, was hard to find.

By the grace of God, in the latter half of the twentieth century, reformed expository preaching was heard again in British Churches. Pioneers, such as Martin Lloyd-Jones, John Stott, Dick Lucas, James Philip and William Still gave the Bible back to the people of God. Their example and influence awakened a renewed hunger for expository preaching. In the last decades hundreds of faithful preachers have been raised up to build the church on the living Word.

And yet there are disturbing signs that a new famine is by no means out of the question. One of the factors which emerged in parallel with the growth of expository preaching in the post-World War Two era was a flourishing of evangelical scholarship. We now have a vast and growing body of biblically faithful scholarship, which is God's gift to those who preach. However, as evangelicalism gains a seat at the scholarly table some sections of it are in danger of losing their identity. Witness the controversies over open theism, penal substitution, a creeping universalism and a less than firm commitment to the absolute authority of Scripture. As these filter through into evangelical pulpits, we are in danger once more of robbing the Word of God of its authority and thus looking to other things to reach the world and build the church. Biblical capital is not an endless resource; like manna it must be fresh and new every day.

Amos' message here is starkly simple: abandon the Word of God and you lose touch with him. That message applies equally today. When the life-giving Word is lost, the result is spiritual death. We need to see and heed the warning signs.

General Comments

This chapter is important for the theology of judgement which runs through it. A number of points can be made.

Judgement is fair

The wealthy and powerful have deliberately set out to destroy the poor and vulnerable. Thus they have placed themselves in opposition to God. They deny the covenant and run their lives for purely selfish ends.

Judgement is inevitable

The inevitability of judgement is shown by the repetition of 'declares the Lord God' (vv. 3, 9, 11), where the Word of judgement, like the Word of creation, is not simply an announcement of what will happen but the initiating of that process. It is indeed part of the created order like the basket of summer fruit.

Judgement results in the withdrawal of God's Word

Long ago Saul searched for a word from God and did not receive it (1 Sam. 28:6); this was a direct result of his ignoring the Word of God through Samuel. Here this is happening to the whole nation. No nation, no church, no individual can prosper when God's Word is withdrawn.

Preaching and Teaching Notes

Once again, the structure of the chapter suggests a clear structure for a sermon or Bible study on this passage. The overarching theme is the inevitability of judgement. God's people had reached the point of no return. The key application is what this judgement will mean – a famine of the Word of God.

Title: **'A Famine of the Word of God'**
The inevitable consequence of judgement

Text: **Amos 8:1-14**
Structure:

1.   **The Basket of Ripe Fruit: Ripe for Judgement** (*vv. 1-3*)
2.   **Judgement and its Implications** (*vv. 4-14*)
      (i)   Indictment: false religion and injustice (*vv. 4-6*)
      (ii)   Verdict: God judges (*vv. 7-10*)
      (iii) Punishment: a famine of the Word (*vv. 11-14*)

A different approach would be to take it as a sermon on universal guilt, illustrating Romans 3:19: 'so that every mouth may be stopped, and the whole world held to be accountable to God'. Looking at the chapter in this way would suggest a title such as '**Everyone Guilty**' or '**Nothing to Say in Our Defence**' with the following structure.

1. **Nature Condemns Us** *(vv. 1-3) (pointing out similarities to Isaiah 1:3: 'the Ox… and donkey know, but Israel does not know'.)*

2. **The Covenant Condemns Us** *(vv. 4-10) (pointing out how greed and injustice violate the heart of God's self-revelation.)*

3. **God's Word Condemns Us** *(vv. 11-14) (pointing out how the lack of a Word from God leads to death.)*

Equally, we might turn these negatives into positives.

1. **Learn from Creation** *(vv. 1-3)*

2. **Learn from History** *(vv. 4-10)*

3. **Learn from the Word** *(vv. 11-14)*

10

'IN ANGER REMEMBERING MERCY'

Annihilation and restoration

(AMOS 9:1-15)

Introduction

Amos closes his prophecy with a final climactic vision of judgement and announcement of Israel's destruction (9:1-10), followed by a closing oracle of restoration for the faithful remnant (9:11-15). As previously noted, an appropriate final sermon on the prophecy takes these two sections together, under the general theme, 'In Anger Remembering Mercy'.

Throughout Amos, the Lord – rather than Assyria – has been seen as the agent of judgement. Now he appears directly and, in this final vision, the prophet is given a glimpse of the Judge poised to carry out the promised judgement. The vision is introduced: 'I saw the Lord' as opposed to, 'This is what the Lord God showed me' (7.1); a phrase which will be used by Isaiah of his overwhelming encounter with Yahweh (Isa. 6.1). We are face to face here with the sovereignty of Yahweh and this is no longer a time for dialogue; it is the time for judgement.

Vision 5: Yahweh Standing by the Altar at Bethel (9:1-10)

The finality of the judgement and its inescapability and fairness

Notice again the characteristic combination of the visual and the verbal. The vision of the Lord (v. 1a) is followed immediately by a report of what he said (vv. 1b-4; 7-10), which is both in the form of command and statement about the inescapability of judgement. Embedded within this vision of the Lord speaking is Amos' third and final doxology (9:5-6). A number of themes and motifs link this final vision with the opening part of the book and we shall comment on these as we work through the verses. The removal of access to God is at the heart of the vision. Yahweh is not standing at the altar to receive worship or to bless, he is there to destroy; the Creator summons the forces of nature to destroy this idolatrous shrine. The earthquake which has ominously hovered over the land (1:1; 2:13; 3:14-15; 6:11; 8:8) is unleashed and from top to bottom the sanctuary collapses in total ruin. This is no enemy attack where we might expect destruction to begin from the foundations upwards. No longer will the people be able to seek Bethel (5:4). It is not clear exactly to whom the commands 'strike' and 'shatter' are addressed, but clearly God is the agent, and it may be that the words spoken by Amos are the beginning of that divine Word which has the power both to destroy and create. The people had laid much emphasis on their shrines (see ch. 5) but now the Lord himself has destroyed their means of access to him just as he has sent a famine of hearing his words (7:11-14). The God who would have longed to meet his people in grace now destroys the temple at Bethel.

God's judgement is inescapable (9:2-4)

The way of access to God by the Temple has now been closed and there is no one who can evade God's judgement. No part of creation can provide a hiding place from the Creator, as Adam and Eve discovered when they tried to hide from him (Gen. 3:8). The language here recalls Psalm 139:7-11 but with the emphasis on terror rather than security. There is no refuge to be found either in Sheol, the land of the dead, or in heaven, God's dwelling place, Carmel, already mentioned in 1:2 as withering at the roar of the lion, is the highest point in the land and yet, like the bottom of the sea, is totally accessible to God. Even Leviathan (v. 3) will obey Yahweh's will and destroy the fleeing people. Similarly, there is no military or political refuge (v. 4) because the weapons of their enemies will be God's instruments of destruction. God's eye will rest on them but 'for evil and not for good' (v. 4b).

Final doxology (9:5-6)
The nature of God

Embedded within this vision of the Lord speaking from the altar at Bethel is the third and final of Amos' doxologies (vv. 5-6). The key note of Amos' final doxology is that God's judgement is wholly consistent with God's character. Yahweh, the Warrior, has power to carry out what he says he will do. The great doctrines of creation and providence which lie at the heart of the Old Testament are very far from being abstract theories. Positively, they mean that people can build their lives securely on the Rock, knowing that the One who made them is the One who will guide them throughout their lives and complete the good work he has begun. Negatively, as here, they mean that the Creator and

Lord of History will punish those who flout his laws and despise his Word. At the Exodus the waters were driven back to secure the safety of God's people. There, as Yahweh the Warrior, he routed Pharaoh and the gods of Egypt and brought his people out of the land of slavery. He is master of earth and sea and we notice the echo of Psalm 46 which emphasizes Yahweh's protection of his people. Verse 6 is not easy to translate. The 'upper chambers' and 'vault' may refer to the higher and lower storeys of the cosmic temple, but the point that matters is that Yahweh is present and active in all parts of the universe; verbs like 'builds' and 'founds' indicate that his rule is firmly established.

This God is Yahweh; we are left in no doubt of this for his name is repeated at the beginning and end of the doxology. He is the One whose Day is foreshadowed in the judgement about to fall on Israel. Yet in that name is also a glimmer of hope; Yahweh is the Lord of the Covenant and we are about to see how he will remain loyal to that covenant.

The continued pronouncement of judgement (9:7-10)

This oracle takes the form of two rhetorical questions which warn against a false view of election and special relationship. The atmosphere is similar to that of chapter 3:1-8, where the people had used their own election as a guarantee that they were immune from judgement. What is said here is consistent with many of the themes in the 'Oracles Against the Nations' (1:3-2:16) and reinforces that earlier material as the prophecy draws to a conclusion. It is, however, no mere repetition; this is a call for a thorough reappraisal of their historic relationship with God, and consequently, of the practical implications for their behaviour and understanding of who God is.

Two things in particular call for comment. The first is that Yahweh's writ runs over the whole earth (v. 7). This was not a denial of the covenant with Israel but the context necessary for it. It means that in one sense being an Israelite is no more of a privilege than being English, Scottish or Australian! Yet it is also no less. Yahweh is not revoking the covenant nor denying the fact that he brought them out of Egypt. It is salutary for them to learn that God also brought about the migrations of hostile neighbours, the Philistines and the Syrians, as well as caring for the people of remote Ethiopia (Cush). This is another devastating indictment of their pride and complacency. The Exodus was hugely important, but merely to remember it without thanksgiving, awe and worship is akin to the wholly secular exploitation of Christmas. The event itself simply remains an episode in the past unless it transforms the lives of those who look back to it. The privileges have not been withdrawn, but at this point, because of the great revelation they have been given, Israel is worse off and liable to greater judgement than anyone else.

The second principle is developed in verses 8-10. A remnant will survive the judgement. Even when the whole nation is justly condemned, there is a way of escape for those who have heeded the prophet's earlier warnings and sought the Lord. The metaphor of the sieve recalls that of the plumb line (7:7-8) because both separate true from false, leaving only that which is authentic after the judgement. This is underlined by two expressions: 'I will not utterly destroy the house of Jacob' (v. 8) and 'All the sinners of my people shall die by the sword, who say, "Disaster shall not overtake or meet us"' (v. 10). The first statement has been anticipated in 5:15: 'it may be that the Lord, the God of hosts, will be gracious to the remnant of Joseph'. The second statement indicates a differentiation with regard to sinners, and points specifically to those who remain stubborn and complacent with no sense of God's impending judgement. The true Israel, while still sinners, are those who are actively seeking God and striving to live lives of holiness.

There is much here that is of huge importance in our thinking about the gospel and how we preach it. We must never think that salvation is different in the Old and New Testaments. Faith and living by that faith is the only way to life (see Heb. 11) and that is what is happening here. There are two implications. One is that foreigners can become part of the covenant community if they obey the Covenant Lord (Rahab and Ruth are outstanding examples). The other implication is that simply because someone is genetically an Israelite, that does not make them spiritually a believer. Paul makes this very plain when he says: 'For not all who are descended from Israel belong to Israel' (Romans 9:6). Here the concept of the remnant becomes vital because, through them, God's covenant with the whole people will be realized.

As we preach on this there is much that can be said on the latter-day remnant within the professing church. This is an issue particularly, but by no means exclusively, for those who minister in national churches, where the local church is seen by many people as 'their' church, even though they have had no experience of saving faith. Amos here gives us a clear model: judgement is inevitable, but there is a way of escape for those who seek the Lord and turn to him.

All of Amos' preaching is God-centred. In his doxologies especially, he has shown a wonderful sense of the magnificence of the Creator and the wonder of his work.

Moreover, he has demonstrated God's intimate involvement in human affairs and the inevitability of his judgements. Nor is his judgement an abstract force; a past relationship will not be an immunity badge if there is indulgence in sin.

Closing Oracle of Restoration (9:11-15)

The glorious future and the bright day beyond the night of judgement

The long tunnel is over and we emerge into glorious sunlight. So vivid is the contrast that many have felt that this final section cannot be by Amos but is the work of a post-exilic writer who wants to end the book on a positive note. Such a view hardly stands up to examination. If this was indeed a later author he was remarkably naïve in preparing so inadequately for his happy ending. In fact, the transition from verse 10 to verse 11 is not as abrupt as it seems. Let me explain.

Has Amos lost the plot?

No one can deny that the book has been full of judgement, but a careful reading will find that right from the beginning Amos has emphasized the faithfulness of God and the hope that is available for all who turn to him. At the outset, the God whose terrifying roar is heard throughout the land is none other than the Lord himself. This, as we noted, is also emphasized in the final doxology (9:5-6). Thus God remains faithful to the covenant first made with Abraham (Gen. 15 and 17) and reaffirmed to Isaac (Gen. 26:24-25) and to Jacob (Gen. 35:9-15). The Sinai Covenant was made with Moses on behalf of the whole people at Sinai (Exod. 19 and 20), embodied in the Decalogue, further developed in the Book of the Covenant (Exod. 20:22–23:33) and further spelled out in Deuteronomy. The Davidic Covenant (2 Sam. 7)

speaks of the eternal throne of David's descendants. This
covenant relationship explains both the necessity for and
severity of judgement for violations, with ultimate salvation
for the faithful.

Other signs of ultimate hope which spring from the
covenant are scattered throughout the book. The fact that
the Lord roars not only from Jerusalem but from Zion (1:2)
reminds us of his eternal choice of his dwelling place. We
have already noted that the preaching of judgement is also
a call to repentance (see e.g. 4:12; 5:14-15, 24) with Amos
in a Moses-like role as intercessor (7:2,5). The possibility
of salvation, therefore, has been held out throughout the
prophecy. Amos goes on now to show us a glimpse of what
future salvation will mean.

The nature of this oracle

This closing oracle is a revelation of the future. The phrases 'in
that day' (v. 11) and 'Behold, the days are coming' (v. 13) show
us that this is an eschatological passage. Clearly, the return from
exile is a provisional and partial fulfilment, but the absence
of a Davidic king and the stringent economic conditions (see
Hag. 1:4; 9-11; Mal. 3:9-11) hardly fit the glowing picture
of exuberant abundance. The tone is joyful and poetic and
another fine example of Amos' colourful, pictorial style.

The passage can be compared with many other prophetic
glimpses of the future: Isaiah 11–12; 24; 35; Ezekiel 40–
48; Zephaniah 3:14-20 and Zechariah 14. Each of these
prophets sees the time to come as embodying and perfecting
what they most value in both past and present and what
fits best with the overall direction of their message. Here,
Amos re-emphasizes the three great concerns identified as
his 'theme tune' back in 1:1-2: God as Lord of History; God

as Lord of Creation and the God who Speaks. The message is consistent because God is consistent. We shall look at each of these in turn.

(1)   God is Lord of History

History will reach its climax, not in the sense that nothing more will happen, but that it will become uniquely the continuing development of God's relationship with his people in the new heaven and new earth. This has implications both for Israel and the other nations (again recalling chs. 1 and 2). Verses 11 and 12 speak of the restoration of the Davidic kingdom and the effect of this on the nations.

'The booth of David' (v. 11a) is an interesting expression, discussed in full in the larger commentaries. It clearly refers to the restoration of the Davidic house, but 'house' is not used and we need to think through the implications of using the word 'booth'. The most common use of the word in the Old Testament is in connection with the Feast of Booths (see Lev. 23:42). Linking this with David joins the two great Old Testament figures of Moses and David, giving a sense of continuity and fulfilment. True worship and true kingship, so conspicuously absent in Amos' day, will flourish in the Messianic Age. All that was good and godly will come to glorious fruition. Repairing breaches and rebuilding ruins may refer to the reuniting of the two kingdoms (Ezek. 37:15-28).

Other nations will be involved as well, and these are included under the phrase 'the remnant of Edom' (v. 12a). Edom is particularly appropriate after the references to Jacob (7:2, 5). The ruptured relationship of the descendants of these two is to be finally healed. It is fascinating to see how in Acts 15:12-19 this is the passage used by James to show that the Gentiles are co-heirs with the Jews of the grace of God. How spectacularly and gloriously is Amos' prophecy to be fulfilled.

(2)   God is Lord of Creation

Creation will be renewed because the coming Son of David is also the last Adam who will remove the curse of Genesis 3 and bring in a new heaven and new earth. After many grim references to drought and famine (e.g. 1:2; 4:6-7) Amos now looks forward to an abundant and fertile earth which was only foreshadowed in the land of milk and honey. Indeed, the mountains and hills will appear to be awash with wine. This is an enormously important truth. In a sense the rest of the Bible is an unfolding of Genesis 1:1: 'In the beginning, God created the heavens and the earth'. Our (present) sinful world appears to suggest that he did not succeed, but Amos, with the other prophets, point to a coming day when creation will be brought to glorious fulfilment for all eternity.

There is an important issue here. It is often argued (particularly in liberal scholarship) that prophets were 'forth-tellers' rather than 'foretellers' and were primarily concerned with their own day. This might account for attempts to prune out passages such as this. However, the reason the prophets were able to speak so powerfully and effectively to their own day was that they spoke from the perspective of eternity and thus had a lasting message not only for their own but all other ages. Amos was able to preach judgement and exile and the call for repentance because he knew that the Day of Yahweh would certainly come. The covenant would be wonderfully fulfilled and sin and death would be gone.

The picture of the fertile earth merges into one of the people returning to their land to rebuild cities, plant vineyards and enjoy all the blessings of peace. This is once again a passage that speaks of the return from exile but goes far beyond that to the blessings of the new creation. Likewise, it uses the metaphor of the vine (Psalm 80:8ff; Isaiah 5:1-11) and planting in general with the sense both of roots and shoots. God is keeping his ancient promises. The gift of land was at the heart of the covenant with Abraham and is a firm reminder that the new heaven and earth will be real places; we do not look for some kind of disembodied existence in a shadow land.

(3) *God Speaks*

The Word of God will bring all this about. This is another great theme which has run through Amos. Here it appears three times (vv. 12, 13 and 15). God speaks and he brings both blessing and judgement by his words. These words of Amos are not his imaginary account of a hypothetical future; they are the words of God who has committed himself to his people by promises which he cannot and will not break. The people are 'my' people and Yahweh speaks of himself as 'your God'.

Amos has thus reinforced the main themes of his book in a way which does justice to the full seriousness of his message. There is hope, but only those who seek the Lord will find it, and when they do they will discover that this Lord is no unknown power but the One who has been completely faithful to them. The future hope of Israel has its roots in the call to the patriarchs, the events of the Exodus and further back still in God's gracious creation of the heavens and the earth.

Preaching and Teaching Notes

As Amos draws together the different strands of his argument in this final chapter, so also our final sermon or Bible study on the book, should draw together the series of studies to the appropriate conclusion. The final sermon on Amos will be reinforcement of many of the major themes already covered as well as an opportunity to place these in the context of God's ongoing purposes.

The most obvious way to preach a sermon on this final chapter would be to take the two main divisions, and use a title such as 'In Anger Remembering Mercy' or 'The Goodness and Severity of God'. In the structure below (reflecting the structure of Amos 9), the two main points dealing with judgement and mercy are bracketed with references to God speaking through his Word. This reflects Amos' emphasis (both in this closing chapter and in the prophecy as a whole) that God's Word is central to both judgement and blessing.

Title: **'In Anger Remembering Mercy'**
Annihilation and restoration

Text: **Amos 9:1-15**
Structure:

God Speaks (*v. 1*)
1.   **Where God Judges…** (*vv. 1-10*)
      (i)   We will not escape (*vv. 1-4*)
      (ii)   We will recognize who he is (*vv. 5-6*)
      (iii)   We will not be able to claim any special relationship (*vv. 7-10*)

2.   **When God Blesses…** (*vv. 11-15*)
      (i)   He will complete his purposes in history (*vv. 11-12*)
      (ii)   He will renew his creation (*vv. 13-15*)

God Has Spoken (*vv. 12-15*)

ADDITIONAL MATERIAL

11

A THEMATIC LOOK AT AMOS

Introduction

The principal focus of this book has been to explore the text of Amos, identifying both the main thrust of the prophecy and how Amos shapes his material. This is the right approach and should always be our primary focus in preaching. The danger of thematic preaching, as pointed out in chapter 1, is that the preacher can abstract ideas from their setting and present them in a way which robs them of their power. However, having studied the book, there is value in looking at some of the main themes, not least because it will help to fix in our minds the main concerns of the prophet. Five main themes are suggested.

(1) Amos' God

Amos' God dominates the book and is presented in a number of ways. The first picture of God is intensely dramatic as he 'roars from Zion' (1:2); this God demands our attention immediately. Any trivial or sentimental thoughts we may cherish about God are instantly dismissed. This God is not a stranger; he is already identified as God the Warrior in Exodus 15:3, who is 'majestic in holiness, awesome in glorious deeds, doing wonders' (Exod. 15:11).

He is presented as the agent of judgement. For example, it is striking the number of times 'I' is the subject of the verbs of destruction in chapters 1 and 2. Assyria, the main human actor, is not mentioned because Amos is concerned to emphasize the total sovereignty of Yahweh. Similarly, at the end, God is the sole agent in prosperity and the time of unparalleled blessing.

God is inescapable (see esp. 9:1-4) and everything in heaven and earth is related to him. There is no power beyond him to which appeal can be made; he alone carries out his promises to save and judge.

He is Yahweh, the Lord of the Covenant who 'knows' his people (3:2). He does not overlook their sin but provides a way of escape for the remnant who remain faithful to his commands. Amos is categorical in his emphasis that God's people are under judgement, not because God has broken his covenant, but because they have been unfaithful. Here is a great opportunity to preach on the unconditional love of God as well as showing that when such love is appreciated, it results in lives of holiness not sinfulness. All that Amos says begins with the living God, is dominated by him and shaped by him. That is equally essential in our preaching, so that we can address people's real needs and bring truth that is life-changing. In a real sense, God is Amos' theme and the other four 'sub-themes' flow from this.

(2) The Worship of God

Amos has two basic themes here: true and false worship. True worship is embodied in the four doxological passages

(1:2; 4:13; 5:8-9; 9:5-6). These emphasize the awesomeness of God: the lion, the treader on the heights of the earth, the creator of the stars and the Lord of flood and earthquake. But they also show his on-going involvement in his creation at all times and in all places. There is less in Amos about idolatry than in some of the other prophets, for example, Hosea and Isaiah. Rather, he so emphasizes the power and inescapability of Yahweh as to make idolatry unthinkable. The doxological language is powerful; Amos is not simply stating truths about God, he is deeply moved by God's greatness and majesty. So it must be in our preaching; theology and doxology belong together.

The true worship of God is in sharp contrast to the bogus worship attacked by Amos. As already noted, this is marked not so much by idolatry as by flippant and thoughtless use of divinely appointed festivals and a superstitious reverence for sacred places (5:21-24). There is also a chilling disregard for others and ultimately a contempt for the Lord himself (8:4-6). All this springs from a failure to recognize who God is or to prepare to meet him (4:12). God is not Lord of life but simply the 'religious' part of it. Such a 'god' is futile, irrelevant and soon becomes boring. False worship is ultimately self-worship.

(3) The Word of God

God's Word is another major emphasis of Amos, not only at the beginning and end, but throughout the prophecy. Amos makes extensive use of the *messenger formula*: 'declares the Lord' or 'thus says the Lord'. The background to this is the messenger who, having stated his credentials, brings an authoritative message. Amos proclaims the message; he did not make it up. Nevertheless, the style is distinctively his, and marked by powerful imagery and eloquent phraseology. The Word of the Lord comes to 8th century BC Israel through the words of Amos but also to every other century and community. In a real sense the Word becomes flesh in the prophet and must become so in the preacher.

Amos had a difficult message to deliver and one for which he did not volunteer. This comes to light in two particular passages. Chapter 3:3-8, with its series of questions, culminates in the declaration that when the lion roars – when the Lord speaks – he cannot but prophesy. Similarly, in 7:15 Amos tells Amaziah that he has been chosen by God to speak his message. It is just such a blend of reluctance and compulsion which lies at the heart of speaking for God, and all genuine preachers will experience it. Amos is the servant of the Word of God and all the evident rhetorical skills with which he has been gifted are used to present that message fully and clearly. This Word cannot be resisted and, while it may be ignored for a time, cannot be evaded forever.

As preachers we need to recover a true sense of the power and authority of the living Word of God. We do not have to make it relevant. What we need to do is preach it in such a way as to allow it to demonstrate its own total relevance.

(4) Amos' Social Concern

Amos' social concern and emphasis on justice is a major theme throughout the whole book. It shows first in the 'Oracles against the Nations' (chs. 1 and 2) where cruelty (e.g. 1:6) and oppression (e.g. 2:6-7) are some of the evils that the Lord condemns. It continues in the denunciation of the extravagant lifestyle of the rich (3:1; 6:1-6) and the condemnation of systemic corruption (5:10-11; 8:4-6). Amos is in no doubt that these social conditions were the product of sin and greed.

Amos gives us an effective model of how to preach on those issues. Evangelicals are often nervous about appearing to preach a 'social gospel' and can, in consequence, sometimes appear to be uncaring about such matters. This is usually an unfair view because most evangelicals care deeply about the poor and oppressed. Indeed, one of the results of faithful Word ministry will not only produce people committed to such ministries, but will inspire others to work with street children, help villagers, to dig wells and work for famine relief. But how do we preach on these themes? We cannot preach on this book without engaging with these issues.

Some suggestions have already been made in comments on the relevant passages, but one or two things ought to be said here. Amos links social justice with the nature of God. The God whom Israel claims to worship is merciful and just, and his followers must show these same qualities in their lives. Treatment of widows and orphans flows from a relationship with the God who cares for the weak and avenges the downtrodden. It is not an alternative way of having such a relationship; rather, it is one of the fruits of the relationship.

Also, this concern for social justice springs from the Torah and thus shows obedience to the Word of God. Chapter 4 echoes the covenant curses of Deuteronomy 28 and is a powerful reminder of how the Torah governs the whole of life and is not simply for 'religious' activities. This is linked to the conviction that the Lord is one and that there is no area of heaven and earth where his writ does not run and his Word is not relevant. To preach on issues of justice in this context is not to preach another gospel, but rather to demonstrate that the true gospel has social implications.

(5) Amos' Visions

Amos' reporting of visions is another important theme, referred to in 1:1: 'The words of Amos ... which he saw concerning Israel', and developed fully in the visions of chapters 7-9. Once again, these have important implications for preaching, not least in a culture where the Word is increasingly devalued. It needs to be emphasized that Word and vision are not alternatives. The vision is that sight of true reality which is given to the prophet who then expounds it in words. Amos is not asked to draw a picture of what he has seen but to tell it. And the words he uses will be either life or death for those who hear. These words are, as we have seen, vivid, full of illustration and analogy and engage all aspects of personality.

The task of the preacher, like that of the prophet, is to open people's eyes to reality and help them see that reality for themselves. Hence the repeated use of metaphor, illustration, story and analogy. We must not set up an allegedly interesting visual presentation against an allegedly boring verbal one. Doubtless there is boring preaching – too much of it – but that is the result not of any deficiency in the living Word of God but of the failure of the preacher to engage reverently and imaginatively with it. In his visions, Amos is not merely an observer, he is engaged as intercessor and preacher and from this his authority derives. These visions are closely linked to the setting in which Amos is speaking.

The aim of this short chapter has been to underline the main emphases of Amos and give some indication of how they are developed throughout his book. This approach might be the basis for a final sermon in a series on Amos or the basis for a number of group Bible studies. It does not aim to be an alternative to the systematic exposition of the book, but rather to show an example of how we might explore it thematically.

Appendix

FURTHER RESOURCES FOR
TEACHING AMOS

This book is not a commentary in the sense of fully expounding the text of Amos and giving detailed justifications for all the interpretations suggested. Nor is it a series of sermons on Amos. Rather it gives guidance and encouragement to those who want to preach and teach Amos, but are uncertain how to go about it. There are many commentaries on Amos and the purpose of this Appendix is to give some guidance on these and particularly to commend some which I have found useful and stimulating. It is important to remember that commentaries are not simply good because they are 'sound' or bad because they take critical positions with which we may not be in agreement. No commentary will be helpful on every passage.

Recognize commentaries for what they are: resources to help us to understand the text accurately so that we can expound it effectively. I will divide the commentaries into different categories and make a few comments on each. It hardly need be said that these selections are simply my personal choice, but they may be of some help in guiding you to the best resources.

Commentaries

Large scale: *The Anchor Bible Commentary* by **Francis I. Andersen and David I. Freedman** (Doubleday, 1989) with its lengthy introduction and 977 pages is not for the faint-hearted. However, if you want to study at least parts of the prophet in detail this book is essential, especially if you want guidance on the Hebrew text. Probably less daunting – and certainly more serviceable for the preacher – is *The Mentor Commentary* by **Gary V. Smith** (Christian Focus 1998; earlier edn. by Zondervan 1989). This is a thorough, careful and illuminating exposition.

Medium: **David Allen Hubbard** produced the *Tyndale Commentary*, which also includes Joel (IVP 1989). This is a well-written, detailed and insightful commentary of great use to the preacher. (You also get his fine commentary on Joel, so this is a bargain.) **Alec Motyer's** *BST Volume* (IVP 1974) is a fine model of how to move from exegesis to exposition with the main critical issues covered in exceptionally useful footnotes.

Shorter: Many commentaries deal with several of the prophets in one volume. Some of these are worth mentioning. **Thomas E. McComiskey** has edited three volumes on *The Book of the Twelve* (Baker 1992) and the commentary on Amos is written by **Jeffrey Nichaus**. It is good on the Hebrew text and on background. **Peter Craigie** in *The Twelve Prophets* (DSB 2 Vols. 1985) comments on Amos in vol. 1 and has some useful applications. **Douglas Stuart** comments on Amos in the *Word Bible Commentary* (vol. 1 Amos-Jonah) (WBC. 1987) and has some valuable observations on theology.

Other Resources

There are some helpful works on the prophets and prophecy in general. **William Van Generen's** *Interpreting the Prophetic Word* (Zondervan 1990) is a lucid overview of the prophetic literature and has a useful chapter on Amos. **Mary Evan's** *Prophets of the Lord* (Paternoster 1992) is a straightforward introduction. An older work, *Men Spake From God* by **Howard Ellison** (Paternoster 1952 - later reprints) has still many valuable insights.

Students of the prophets would benefit from a good knowledge of historical background. **David F. Payne's** *Kingdoms of the Lord* (Paternoster 1981) has a useful section on the prophets. **Iain Provan, V. Phillips Long and Tremper Longman III**, three conservative scholars, have produced a helpful book, *A Biblical History of Israel* (Westminster 2003) which deals cogently with recent attack on the historicity of the Old Testament.

Generally speaking, a useful rule when preaching on a book is to consult at least three commentaries of different kinds and to learn from a wide variety of insights. My pick on Amos would be Hubbard, Motyer and Smith.

Christian Focus Publications

publishes books for all ages

Our mission statement –

STAYING FAITHFUL

In dependence upon God we seek to help make His infallible Word, the Bible, relevant. Our aim is to ensure that the Lord Jesus Christ is presented as the only hope to obtain forgiveness of sin, live a useful life and look forward to heaven with Him.

REACHING OUT

Christ's last command requires us to reach out to our world with His gospel. We seek to help fulfill that by publishing books that point people towards Jesus and help them develop a Christ-like maturity. We aim to equip all levels of readers for life, work, ministry and mission.

Books in our adult range are published in three imprints.

Christian Focus contains popular works including biographies, commentaries, basic doctrine and Christian living. Our children's books are also published in this imprint.

Mentor focuses on books written at a level suitable for Bible College and seminary students, pastors, and other serious readers. The imprint includes commentaries, doctrinal studies, examination of current issues and church history.

Christian Heritage contains classic writings from the past.

Christian Focus Publications, Ltd
Geanies House, Fearn, Ross-shire,
IV20 1TW, Scotland, United Kingdom
info@christianfocus.com
www.christianfocus.com